CONTEMPORARY

INTERMEDIATE 1 READER

reading basics

A REAL-WORLD APPROACH TO LITERACY

Bothell, WA • Chicago, IL • Columbus, OH • New York, NY

Image Credits: Cover Lisa Fukshansky/The McGraw-Hill Companies; **1** (c)The Field Museum, GN87713_7c.; **10** Mary Lightfine; **18** AP Photo; **26** AP Photo/Bob Broadbeck; **34** Bruce Gilbert/MCT/Newscom; **41** Art Media/Photolibrary; **49** THE CANADIAN PRESS/Peter Bregg/AP Photo; **57** Charles Hewitt/Picture Post/Hulton Archive/Getty Images; **65** Visuals Unlimited/CORBIS; **73** Fotosearch/Getty Images; **81** Patrick Robert/Sygma/CORBIS; **89** Comstock Images/PunchStock; **97** Royalty-Free/CORBIS; **105** MPI/Getty Images; **113** ABPL/DE LA HARPE, ROGER/Animals Animals-Earth Sciences.

www.mheonline.com

Copyright © 2012 by The McGraw-Hill Companies, Inc.

All rights reserved. No part of this publication may be reproduced or distributed in any form or by any means, or stored in a database or retrieval system, without the prior written consent of The McGraw-Hill Companies, Inc., including, but not limited to, network storage or transmission, or broadcast for distance learning.

Send all inquiries to:
Contemporary/McGraw-Hill
130 East Randolph Street, Suite 400
Chicago, IL 60601

ISBN: 978-0-07-659101-5
MHID: 0-07-659101-8

Printed in the United States of America.

1 2 3 4 5 6 7 8 9 QLM 15 14 13 12 11

Contents

To the Student.................................... v

UNIT 1

Lesson 1.1
The Man-Eaters of Tsavo............................ 1

Lesson 1.2
Doctors (and Nurses) Without Borders 10

Lesson 1.3
The Truth about the Tasaday 18

Lesson 1.4
Near Death on the Football Field................... 26

Lesson 1.5
The Mysterious Life of Twins....................... 34

UNIT 2

Lesson 2.1
Mummies... 41

Lesson 2.2
Escape from Iran 49

Lesson 2.3
Alone at Sea....................................... 57

Lesson 2.4
Night Killers 65

Lesson 2.5
Escape to Freedom.................................. 73

UNIT 3

Lesson 3.1
A Horrible Way to Die............................. 81

Lesson 3.2
A Shocking Experience 89

Lesson 3.3
Needles That Cure 97

Lesson 3.4
Hanging from a Cliff 105

Lesson 3.5
Killer Bees 113

Words-per Minute Table 121

Plotting Your Progress Graph:
Reading Speed 122

To the Student

The articles in this book will introduce you to some intriguing events, people, and animals. All the articles recount actual events. They are all true stories. They will grab your interest and keep you reading to the end. You will learn something from every article. As you read and enjoy them, you will also develop your reading skills.

You will have many unanswered questions after reading the articles. You may be puzzled or amazed. However, you will not be bored. When you finish reading, you will answer questions to check your understanding of the story. You will also apply critical thinking skills to help you connect to what you have read.

If you finish all 15 lessons—reading the articles and completing the exercises—you will surely increase your reading speed and improve your reading comprehension and critical thinking skills. The exercises include questions similar to those in various assessments. Learning how to complete them will prepare you for tests you may take in the future.

There is a recording of each article. Go to www.mhereadingbasics.com to play or download the recordings. The recordings provide modeled fluency and read-along support.

The Reading Extension section of the accompanying *Reading Basics Intermediate 1 Student Edition* relates to the articles. The *Student Edition* presents reading-skill instruction that will help you with your understanding of these articles. You may read the articles or listen to the recordings anytime you wish.

About the Book

Reading Basics Intermediate 1 Reader contains three units, each of which includes five lessons. Each lesson begins with an article about an unusual event, person, group, or animal. A set of six exercises follows each article. The first three reading comprehension exercises will help you better understand the article. These exercises are Recognize and Recall Details, Find the Main Idea, and Summarize and Paraphrase. The next three exercises will assist you in thinking about what you have read and how it relates to your own experience. These exercises are Make Inferences, Recognize Author's Effect and Intentions, and Evaluate and Create.

Working through Each Lesson

Begin each lesson by looking at the photograph and reading the title, the caption, and Before You Read. Next, read the boldface words and their meanings that are in the margins of the article. Then read the article. Finally, complete the exercises. The directions for each exercise tell you how to mark your answers.

Sometimes your teacher may decide to time your reading. Timing helps you keep track of and increase your reading speed. If you have been timed, enter your reading time in the Timed Reading section at the end of the article. Then use the Words-per-Minute Table on page 121 to find your reading speed. Finally, record your speed on the Plotting Your Progress Graph: Reading Speed on page 122.

Reading Basics Intermediate 1 Reader will build your confidence in your ability to read by letting you practice on short, interesting, engaging articles.

Unit 1 · Lesson 1.1

The Man-Eaters of Tsavo

Today the lions that plagued the Tsavo area are mounted and on exhibit at Chicago's Field Museum. They killed more than 120 people during their lifetimes.

Before You Read
Predict

Read the title of the article and the photo caption and look at the photograph. Skim the article. Then predict what will happen.
- Whom will the lions eat?
- How will people try to defend themselves against the lions?

....

The Man-Eaters of Tsavo

1   These days they're harmless. In fact, you can find them mounted and on display at Chicago's Field Museum. But when they were alive, they were a terror. There were only two of them, but they killed at will. People lost sleep worrying about who would be the next victim. One person died of shock just thinking about "the man-eaters of Tsavo."

2   In 1898 the British were building a railroad across east Africa. It was not an easy task. The tracks crossed mile after mile of barren land. Food, water, and supplies had to be hauled in from far away. Skilled workers had to be brought in from the East Indies. Then when the railroad reached the Tsavo River, they faced an even bigger problem. This new problem was lions—two huge lions that fed on human flesh.

3   Colonel John Henry Patterson was in charge of the railroad project. At first he didn't believe the workers' stories of lion attacks. He thought they were just rumors. Then one night he became convinced of the lions' existence. One of the lions snuck into the tent of a railroad worker. The lion grabbed the worker by the throat. As another worker watched in horror, he was **dragged** out of the tent. "Let go!" he cried. But the lion's grip was too strong. The next day, Patterson found the worker's remains. It was not a pretty sight.

dragged
pulled

4   The other workers, of course, were terrified. Many ran away or refused to work. Patterson was scared too. He knew the lions had to be killed. Otherwise, the railroad line would never get finished. Being a skilled hunter, he decided that he would kill them himself. He didn't think it would be that hard to do. He was wrong.

5   That night Patterson, taking his rifle, climbed up into a tree near the area where the worker had been killed. There he waited for the lions. He had tied a goat to the tree, hoping this tasty meal would **entice** them. The lions, however, had a different meal in mind. Late that night, one of the cats attacked another tent, far away from the spot where Patterson was waiting, and dragged away another worker.

entice
attract

6   Patterson heard the victim's screams, but there was little he could do. Work camps stretched for eight miles along the railroad. He couldn't guard them all. Instead, he decided to build thick thorn fences around each camp. He thought that would keep the man-eaters out. The workers felt much safer with the fences in place. They also began keeping a fire burning in each camp throughout the night.

7   None of these safety measures worked, however. The lions never missed a meal. They either jumped over the fences or they crawled through weak spots in them. Once again, the killings terrorized the workers.

8   Patterson was frightened too. "In the whole of my life," he said, "I have never experienced anything more nerve shaking than to hear the deep roars of these dreadful monsters." When the roaring came closer, "I knew that some one or other of us was doomed to be their victim." Just before the lions entered a camp, their roaring **ceased**. That's when the men knew one of the lions was stalking its prey. Soon

ceased
stopped

the beast would attack. But where? Patterson never seemed to guess right. He kept setting traps, but the lions kept striking someplace else. The lions, he later said, always seemed to know where his traps were.

9   At last, Patterson decided to try a new tactic. He would no longer wait for the lions to come to him. He would hunt the lions on their own ground. Day after day, he crawled through the bushes. He never found them. That was probably just as well. If he had come across them, they would almost certainly have killed him before he could kill them.

10   Meanwhile work on the railroad had come to a complete stop. Hundreds of workers had run away. Those who stayed could think of only one thing—how to stay safe. Some tied their beds up in trees. Others slept on the tops of water tanks or roofs. Still others stayed in their tents but dug pits in the middle of the dirt floor. They slept in the pits, which they covered with heavy logs.

11   One day Patterson came across a donkey that the lions had killed. They hadn't eaten all of it, and Patterson thought they might return to finish their meal. So he built a platform near the donkey's body outside one of the camps. That night he sat on the top of the platform with his rifle and waited.

12   Soon one of the lions came near. With no moon, the night was black, and it was difficult to see. But Patterson could hear the lion's deep sigh. The animal was hungry. But it was not going after the donkey. It was going after Patterson! Slowly the lion circled the platform. Patterson sat there terrified, "hardly daring even to blink my eyes."

13   The lion came closer and closer. Still Patterson could not see it. Then at last he saw the lion's faint

form **crouched** under a nearby bush. Patterson pulled the trigger of his rifle. The lion gave a terrific roar. It ran into the thick brush. Patterson kept firing where he thought the lion was hiding. The lion's growls turned to moans. Then the night was silent. One of the man-eaters of Tsavo was dead.

crouched
lying close to the ground

14 The shooting woke up the whole camp. When the workers heard the news, they gave a loud cheer. "Every man in camp came out," said Patterson, "tom toms split the night air, and horns were blown as men came running to the scene." The workers danced the rest of the night away.

15 The dead lion was huge. It measured nearly nine feet in length and three and a half feet in height. (Male lions rarely grow more than eight feet in length and three feet in height.) It took eight men to carry its body to camp.

16 One lion was dead, but there was still one roaming free. For the second lion, Patterson used dead goats as bait. When the lion approached, he shot it in the shoulder. This lion, however, managed to slip away before he could shoot it again. Ten days later, the beast came back to get one of the men sleeping in a tree. This time Patterson was in the right place. He fired shots at the lion but didn't kill it. The next night, Patterson climbed the same tree. When the lion returned, he shot it in the chest. Once again, the lion got away, badly wounded but not dead.

17 In the morning, Patterson went after the lion. He knew it was injured, so he thought it would be easy to hunt it down. He spotted the lion hiding in some bushes. He fired his rifle. He hit the lion, but that didn't stop it from charging. Patterson shot it again and again. Each time the lion tumbled to the ground only to get up and charge once more.

shattered
broken

Finally, its leg **shattered**, the lion could barely move. Patterson killed it with another volley of shots. The lions' reign of terror was over. The workers returned to their jobs. By then, however, "the man-eaters of Tsavo" had claimed more than 120 lives.

....

Timed Reading

If you have been timed while reading this article, enter your reading time below. Then turn to the Words-per-Minute table on page 121 and look up your reading speed (words per minute). Enter your reading speed on the graph on page 122.

Reading Time: Lesson 1.1

_____ : _____
Minutes   Seconds

COMPREHENSION & CRITICAL THINKING SKILLS

A Recognize and Recall Details

How well do you remember the facts in the article? Put an **X** in the box next to the answer that correctly completes each statement about the article.

1. Colonel Patterson became convinced of the existence of the lions when
    - ☐ **a.** he heard the workers' stories.
    - ☐ **b.** he found the remains of one of the workers.
    - ☐ **c.** a lion grabbed him by the throat.
2. In order to protect the workers, Patterson decided to
    - ☐ **a.** build thorn fences around each camp.
    - ☐ **b.** feed goats to the lions.
    - ☐ **c.** build pits in the workers' tents.
3. The workers knew a lion was about to attack them when
    - ☐ **a.** they heard its roar.
    - ☐ **b.** they saw the beast.
    - ☐ **c.** it grew silent.
4. Patterson climbed a tree and tried to attract the lions by
    - ☐ **a.** tying a goat to a tree.
    - ☐ **b.** building a platform.
    - ☐ **c.** roaring like a lion.

B Find the Main Idea

One statement below expresses the main idea of the article. One statement is too broad. Another statement explains only part of the article—it is too narrow. Label the statements using the following key:

M Main Idea	**B** Too Broad	**N** Too Narrow

_____ 1. Two man-eating lions halted work on a railroad in Africa by killing more than 120 people before Colonel Patterson, the man in charge of the railroad project, killed the lions.

_____ 2. When Colonel Patterson was firing at the lions, he was afraid they would kill him.

_____ 3. Man-eating lions terrorized people in Africa in the late 19th century.

C Summarize and Paraphrase

1. Write a summary of paragraph 8 in no more than 25 words.

   _____
   _____
   _____
   _____

2. Summarize paragraphs 11–13 in two or three sentences.

   _____
   _____
   _____
   _____

3. Put an X in the box next to the best paraphrase for the following sentence from the article: "The lions' reign of terror was over."

   ☐ **a.** The lions were no longer a threat to anyone.

   ☐ **b.** The workers were frightened of the lions because Colonel Patterson had not killed them.

   ☐ **c.** There were no more lions left in the entire Tsavo area.

D Make Inferences

When you combine your own experience with information from a text to draw a conclusion that is not directly stated in the text, you are making an inference. The following inferences about the article may or may not be correct. Label the statements using the following key:

C Correct Inference	**F** Faulty Inference

_____ 1. The lions liked to eat human flesh more than the flesh of other animals.

_____ 2. Patterson was not very confident of his hunting skills.

_____ 3. All the railroad workers had guns, but they did not use them because they preferred that Colonel Patterson take the risk himself.

_____ 4. Lions cannot climb trees easily.

_____ 5. The lions of Tsavo were very strong.

E. Recognize Author's Effect and Intentions

Put an X in the box next to the answer.

1. The author uses the first paragraph of the article to
   - ☐ a. get the reader's attention.
   - ☐ b. inform the reader about the lions of Tsavo.
   - ☐ c. describe the lions of Tsavo.
2. The main purpose of the second paragraph is to
   - ☐ a. summarize the article.
   - ☐ b. describe the setting of the article.
   - ☐ c. introduce the characters in the article.
3. Which of the following statements from the article best describes Colonel Patterson's reason for trying to kill the lions?
   - ☐ a. Patterson was at least as scared as the workers.
   - ☐ b. At first he didn't believe the workers' stories.
   - ☐ c. The railroad line needed to get finished.

F. Evaluate and Create

Put an X in the box next to the answer.

1. Which statement below is an opinion?
   - ☐ a. All lions should be put in zoos.
   - ☐ b. Work camps stretched for eight miles along the railroad.
   - ☐ c. The dead lion was larger than a typical lion.
2. From the article, you can conclude that if Colonel Patterson had not killed the lions,
   - ☐ a. someone else would have killed them.
   - ☐ b. the lions would have stopped terrorizing the railroad workers.
   - ☐ c. the railroad would not have been completed.
3. What was the effect of Patterson waiting for the lions near a half-eaten donkey?
   - ☐ a. Another person in the camp was killed.
   - ☐ b. Patterson was able to kill one of the lions.
   - ☐ c. Patterson built a platform near the donkey.

Unit 1 · Lesson 1.2

Doctors (and Nurses) Without Borders

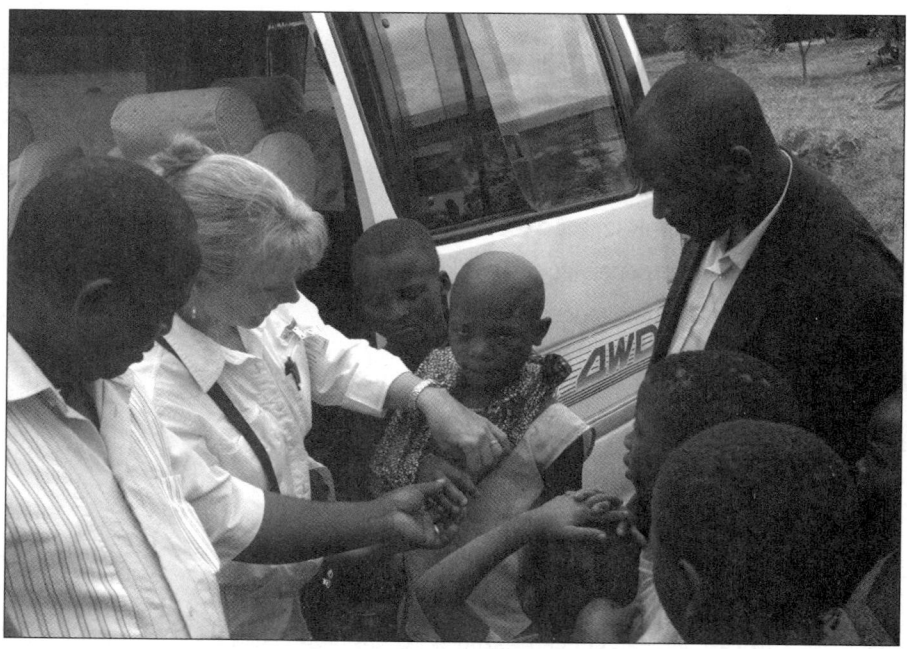

Mary Lightfine, a volunteer with the group Doctors Without Borders, helps a boy with an injured arm in a refugee camp. Doctors Without Borders gives medical care to people in need worldwide.

Ask questions that you would like to find the answers to in the article. For example:

- What does it mean to practice medicine as a doctor or a nurse "without borders"?
- Why do people volunteer for this kind of work?

Before You Read
Ask Questions

1   Mary Lightfine knew the old man was dying. She washed him and gave him some fresh blankets to keep him warm. Then she found a tent where he could lie down. But there was nothing more she could do. Lightfine felt terrible for him. She said, "I kept thinking . . . what a horrible feeling to be dying in a refugee camp."

2   Lightfine was right. It was very sad for the man to die in such **grim** conditions. But it would have been even worse if Lightfine had not been there to help. She was part of a group called Doctors Without Borders. On this day in 1997, she was in a refugee camp in Macedonia. She was there to help war victims from nearby Kosovo.

grim
awful

3   Doctors Without Borders began in the 1970s. It was started by French doctors. They wanted to give medical care to those who needed it most. That included people in **remote** parts of the world. It included those who lived through natural disasters. It also included victims of war. The doctors knew it was **risky** to go to some of these places. But they believed everyone should have medical care, no matter where they lived.

remote
far away

risky
dangerous

4   By the 1990s Doctors Without Borders had become a worldwide group. It had about 2,000 workers in more than 80 countries. These workers came from 45 different nations. They weren't paid for their

Lesson 1.2 · Doctors (and Nurses) Without Borders   11 services. They were volunteers. One of the volunteers was Mary Lightfine.

5   Lightfine had a quiet childhood. She spent many of her early years on a farm in Ohio. So she knew how to feed hens and clean out barns. When she grew up, she wanted more action in her life, so she became an emergency-room nurse.

6   For 16 years Lightfine worked in emergency rooms across the United States. By 1992 she felt ready for a change. She still wanted to help the sick and needy, but she wanted to travel more. She wanted to see other countries and learn about other ways of life. When a friend suggested Doctors Without Borders, Lightfine decided to give it a try.

7   It was a decision that changed her life. Over the next eight years, Lightfine worked for Doctors Without Borders in 10 different countries. She gave children vaccines in Uganda. She handed out food in Sudan. She stitched up wounds in Macedonia.

8   Along the way, Lightfine saw a lot of suffering. On the day she bathed the dying man, she also comforted a woman whose home had been destroyed by war. She bandaged a child who had been hurt in the fighting. "If I move fast and don't think about it, I'll be able to perform my work," she said.

9   Sometimes, though, she could barely believe what she saw. She treated one man who had been beaten by enemy soldiers. Said Lightfine, "From his waist down he was blue like a gym bag. He had been tortured and beaten. In all the emergencies I have worked, I have never seen any person bruised that much. It was very difficult for me to imagine that someone could do that to another person."

physical wounds that were ... also saw people in great ... lost their homes. Others ... killed. Many feared their ... to normal. "Sometimes the ... do is hold their hand,"

... fine often gave out markers. ... tures. She found that was a ... express their feelings. Many ... soldiers with guns. Some ... people being killed.

12   On most days Lightfine was at work by 7 A.M. Often she did not stop until midnight. Even when she did have some free hours, she had no place to relax. Her living space was not exactly **plush**.

plush
fancy

13   In Nicaragua, for instance, Lightfine lived in a tiny house along with several others. "It's very basic," she wrote at the time. "There's no stove or refrigerator, and we're eating only canned food. I'm sleeping on a mat on the floor of a windowless pantry."

14   Lightfine went on to describe the heat. She wrote, "It's so hot here that even sleeping with one sheet and a fan on is uncomfortable. I don't have a thermometer, but it must be near 100 degrees."

15   In Sudan things were even worse. Some of the time she lived in a pup tent. The rest of the time she slept in a mud shelter. Lightfine was the only human in the shelter. But there were plenty of rats to keep her company.

16   Given the **hardships**, it may seem surprising that Lightfine loved her job. But she did. She liked helping people. Beyond that, she found that the people she

hardships
difficulties

treated were always very grateful. Some were so thankful they cried. Others hugged her or gave her special blessings. Some tried to share their last bit of food with her. In Macedonia one woman threw her arms around Lightfine and kissed her. Said Lightfine, "More people have said thank you here than in 10 years of working in an emergency room back home. When people say thank you, you've made a difference. For me, that is the greatest gift."

Timed Reading

If you have been timed while reading this article, enter your reading time below. Then turn to the Words-per-Minute table on page 121 and look up your reading speed (words per minute). Enter your reading speed on the graph on page 122.

Reading Time: Lesson 1.2

_____ : _____
Minutes   Seconds

COMPREHENSION & CRITICAL THINKING SKILLS

A Recognize and Recall Details

Put an **X** in the box next to the answer that correctly completes each statement about the article.

1. Doctors Without Borders was started by
   - ☐ a. Mary Lightfine.
   - ☐ b. a group of French doctors.
   - ☐ c. a worldwide organization.

2. Mary Lightfine became an emergency room nurse because she
   - ☐ a. wanted to travel more.
   - ☐ b. didn't like farm work.
   - ☐ c. wanted more action in her life.

3. The people who work for Doctors Without Borders
   - ☐ a. are well paid.
   - ☐ b. come from more than 80 countries.
   - ☐ c. see a lot of suffering.

4. Lightfine did *not* help people
   - ☐ a. who needed vaccines.
   - ☐ b. to rebuild their homes.
   - ☐ c. who were in emotional pain.

B Find the Main Idea

One of the statements below expresses the main idea of the article. One statement is too broad, and another statement is too narrow. Label the statements using the following key:

M Main Idea	**B** Too Broad	**N** Too Narrow

____ 1. The group Doctors Without Borders gives medical care to victims of war and natural disasters. The workers are volunteers.

____ 2. Mary Lightfine worked with Doctors Without Borders as a nurse for eight years in 10 different countries. In spite of the hardships she experienced, she found her work rewarding.

____ 3. In 1997 Mary Lightfine worked as a nurse in a refugee camp in Macedonia.

C Summarize and Paraphrase

1. Reread paragraph 9 of the article. Write a summary of the paragraph in no more than 25 words on the lines below.

   _____
   _____
   _____

   Next, decide how to shorten the summary to 15 words or less without leaving out any essential information. Write on the lines below.

   _____
   _____
   _____

2. Read the statement from the article. Then read the paraphrase of that statement. Choose the reason that best tells why the paraphrase does not say the same thing as the statement.

   Statement: Many feared their lives would never return to normal.

   Paraphrase: Many were afraid they would never return home.

   ☐ **a.** Paraphrase says too much.
   ☐ **b.** Paraphrase doesn't say enough.
   ☐ **c.** Paraphrase doesn't match the statement.

D Make Inferences

The following inferences about the article may or may not be correct. Label the statements using the following key:

C Correct Inference	**F** Faulty Inference

____ **1.** Many remote areas have no doctors.

____ **2.** Volunteers with Doctors Without Borders choose where they want to work.

____ **3.** Mary Lightfine's family did not approve of her work.

____ **4.** Volunteers with Doctors Without Borders live in conditions similar to those of the people they are helping.

E Recognize Author's Effect and Intentions

Put an X in the box next to the answer.

1. The main purpose of the first paragraph is to
   - ☐ a. introduce the topic of the article.
   - ☐ b. describe a scene in which an old man is dying.
   - ☐ c. entertain the reader.
2. What is the author's purpose in writing "Doctors (and Nurses) Without Borders"?
   - ☐ a. to describe the conditions in refugee camps
   - ☐ b. to describe Mary Lightfine
   - ☐ c. to inform the reader about the group Doctor Without Borders and about Mary Lightfine's work
3. Choose the statement that describes the author's position in paragraph 16.
   - ☐ a. Working for Doctors Without Borders is difficult.
   - ☐ b. In spite of the hardships, working for Doctors Without Borders can be rewarding.
   - ☐ c. People in the United States are not grateful for the medical help they receive.

F Evaluate and Create

Put an X in the box next to the answer.

1. Which sentence expresses a fact?
   - ☐ a. It is rewarding to work for Doctors Without Borders.
   - ☐ b. Lightfine saw other countries and learned about other ways of life.
   - ☐ c. Lightfine's work in the United States was less important than her work with Doctors Without Borders.
2. From the information in the article, you can predict that Mary Lightfine
   - ☐ a. will continue to help others.
   - ☐ b. will not work for Doctors Without Borders again.
   - ☐ c. will work only in the United States in the future.

Unit 1 · Lesson 1.3

The Truth about the Tasaday

Supposed members of a lost Stone Age tribe called the Tasaday are shown in the rugged mountain forests of Mindanao Island in the southern Philippines in 1971. It didn't seem possible that a Stone Age tribe could survive in modern times. And it wasn't possible!

You can look for information about a topic before you read an article. For this article, you can work with classmates to

- find information about the Stone Age.
- find information about the Philippines.

Before You Read
Build Background Knowledge

1   Could a Stone Age tribe survive into the 20th century? It didn't seem possible. By 1970 almost every place on Earth had been fully explored. How could any group be living unnoticed by the rest of the world? But in 1971 an amazing thing happened. A Stone Age tribe was found. The name of the tribe was the Tasaday. Experts everywhere were thrilled by this discovery.

2   How did the Tasaday stay unknown for so long? First, the tribe was tiny. It contained just 26 people. Second, they lived in deep caves. Third, their home was in a rain forest deep in the Philippines. Fourth, they made all the things they needed, so they had no reason to seek outside trading partners.

3   The Tasaday were discovered by a local trapper. He said he came upon them one day while hunting. The trapper told Manuel Elizalde, a Philippine official. Soon the word got out. Several experts came to see the tribe. They were eager to study the Tasaday. After all, these people knew nothing about the modern world. Visiting them was like traveling back in time. It allowed researchers to see how humans had lived long, long ago.

4   *National Geographic* fell in love with the Tasaday. The magazine did several stories on the tribe as it "stepped out of the Stone Age." Then came books, movies, and TV specials. Everyone, it seemed, adored these **innocent** people.

innocent
natural; simple

5   What were the Tasaday like? They wore very little clothing. What they did wear they wove from tree

leaves. They did not know how to grow their own food. They had never seen rice, corn, or sugar. One expert said they could be "the only people in the world today who do not know or use tobacco." The Tasaday kept no **domestic** animals either. They survived by eating wild palms, yams, crabs, and tadpoles. And, of course, the Tasaday had no metal. That is why they were called "Stone Age" people. Their only tools came from stone.

domestic
tame

6   The Tasaday were very peaceful. Their sweet nature won the hearts of all those who saw them. The tribe had no words for "weapon" or "war" or "enemy." As one writer put it, "If our **ancestors** were like the Tasaday, we came from far better stock than I believed." It seemed that these Stone Age people might have a lot to teach the rest of us.

ancestors
those from whom one is descended

7   The goal, then, was to protect the Tasaday. That was Elizalde's job. He was in charge of protecting all the tribes in the Philippines. He did not want the Tasaday's way of life ruined. He feared that would happen if too many people came to visit. So he sent soldiers to guard the caves. Just a few people were allowed in, and first they had to be approved by Elizalde. Because of this rule, few scientists got to see the tribe. That's the way things stayed until 1986.

8   Meanwhile, the Tasaday seemed to look on Elizalde as a god. "Our ancestors told us never to leave this place of ours," said one. "They told us the god of our people would come. Their words have been proven true by the coming of Elizalde." The Tasaday even gave him a new name. It was Mono Dakel de Weta Tasaday. That meant "Great Man, God of the Tasaday."

9   As time passed, rumors began to spread. Some people started to have doubts about the tribe. One person claimed he saw cooked rice being sneaked into

the caves. Others said they saw the Tasaday wearing clothes. Still others maintained they had seen tribe members smoking cigarettes. Few people listened to these reports, however. Belief in the "Stone Age" tribe ran too deep.

10   Then, in 1986, a huge change took place in the Philippines. The old government was swept away. A new, freer one was set up. Even before the old regime ended, Elizalde slipped out of sight. He simply vanished. It was said that he fled the country. He took $35 million with him. It was money that he was supposed to have used to aid tribes like the Tasaday.

11   When the old government crumbled, so did the shield around the Tasaday. Now outsiders could see for themselves who these people really were. A Swiss writer named Oswald Iten went looking for the Tasaday. He found their caves empty. He did, however, find the very same "Stone Age" people a short distance away. They were living in comfortable huts. They were wearing T-shirts and jeans. And they were using metal knives.

12   Iten realized that the whole tribe was nothing but a hoax. The people claiming to be Tasaday really came from two other tribes. These tribes had been part of the modern world for many, many years.

13   Soon others picked up the story. ABC did a TV special. It was called "The Tribe That Never Was." It showed the Tasaday laughing as they looked at photos of themselves from *National Geographic*. Tasaday supporters now faced tough questions. Why were the caves so clean? Where were the crab shells and scraps of food? Even Stone Age tribes had garbage, didn't they?

14   Besides, how could such a small tribe **sustain** itself? Wouldn't the Tasaday have needed spouses

sustain
maintain; keep going

from the outside? Scientists said a tribe living on its own would need at least 400 members, not 26. The Tasaday said they sometimes married people from two other Stone Age tribes, but these other tribes were never found.

established
modern day

15 Finally, the Tasaday caves were only a few miles walk from an **established** village. How come no one from the tribe ever walked there? Had their search for food never brought them near the village? It made no sense—unless the tribe was a fake. One expert called the Tasaday "rain forest clock punchers." They went to work as "cave people" in the morning. At night, after the visitors left, they went back to their village homes.

16 Who was behind this fraud? The finger points to Elizalde. He made lots of money from his scheme to "protect" the Tasaday. The Tasaday agreed to go along with him because they were poor. They were told they could make some money by putting on a show. "Elizalde said if we went naked we'd get money because we'd look poor," one man explained.

17 The Tasaday put on a great act. They fooled everyone for a while. Even the so-called experts fell for the scam. We now know that the Tasaday are not a real Stone Age tribe. If such a tribe does still exist, no one has found it yet.

Timed Reading

If you have been timed while reading this article, enter your reading time below. Then turn to the Words-per-Minute table on page 121 and look up your reading speed (words per minute). Enter your reading speed on the graph on page 122.

Reading Time: Lesson 1.3   _____ : _____

                                                    Minutes   Seconds

COMPREHENSION & CRITICAL THINKING SKILLS

A Recognize and Recall Details

Put an **X** in the box next to the answer that correctly completes each statement.

1. The Tasaday tribe was reported to be discovered by a
   - ☐ **a.** visiting scientist.
   - ☐ **b.** government official.
   - ☐ **c.** local trapper.
2. Observers said the Tasaday ate such things as
   - ☐ **a.** wild palms, yams, crabs, and tadpoles.
   - ☐ **b.** rice, corn, and sugar.
   - ☐ **c.** cheese, eggs, and bacon.
3. Manuel Elizalde was given the job of protecting
   - ☐ **a.** the Tasaday from land grabbers.
   - ☐ **b.** all Philippine tribes from too many visitors.
   - ☐ **c.** researchers of the Tasaday.
4. After the old government crumbled,
   - ☐ **a.** a Swiss writer discovered the Tasaday hoax.
   - ☐ **b.** Manuel Elizalde was arrested.
   - ☐ **c.** the Tasaday had to pay money to the government.

B Find the Main Idea

One of the statements below expresses the main idea of the article. One statement is too broad. The other statement is too narrow. Label the statements using the following key:

M Main Idea	**B** Too Broad	**N** Too Narrow

   ____ 1. Researchers and scientists can be misled when their desire to make remarkable discoveries overcomes their common sense.

   ____ 2. The apparent discovery of a Stone Age tribe in the Philippines in 1971 was revealed to be a hoax just 15 years later.

   ____ 3. Manuel Elizalde, a Philippine official, said that he was protecting a small, primitive tribe from the modern world.

C Summarize and Paraphrase

1. Look for the important ideas and events in paragraphs 3 and 4. Summarize those paragraphs in two or three sentences.

   _____
   _____
   _____
   _____

2. Read the statement from the article. Then read the paraphrase of that statement. Choose the reason that best tells why the paraphrase does not say the same thing as the statement.

   Statement: In 1986 Elizalde vanished, taking $35 million meant for the Tasaday with him.

   Paraphrase: Elizalde disappeared in 1986.

   ☐ **a.** Paraphrase says too much.
   ☐ **b.** Paraphrase doesn't say enough.
   ☐ **c.** Paraphrase doesn't agree with the statement.

D Make Inferences

When you combine your own experience with information from a text to draw a conclusion that is not directly stated in the text, you are making an inference. The following inferences about the article may or may not be correct. Label the statements using the following key:

C Correct Inference	**F** Faulty Inference

_____ **1.** Rain forests cover a large amount of land in the Philippines and are home to many people.

_____ **2.** Scientists do not know much about the daily life of people in the Stone Age.

_____ **3.** All officials in the old Philippine government were dishonest.

_____ **4.** Swiss writers are more careful in their research than other writers.

_____ **5.** If researchers had not been carried away by the idea of making a great discovery, they could have seen that the Tasaday tribe was a fake.

E. Recognize Author's Effect and Intentions

Put an X in the box next to the answer.

1. The main purpose of the first paragraph is to
   - ☐ a. introduce readers to the topic of the article.
   - ☐ b. describe the Tasaday tribe.
   - ☐ c. point out how easily people can be fooled.

2. You can conclude that the author wants the reader to think that
   - ☐ a. no one believed the Tasaday were Stone Age people.
   - ☐ b. many people were fooled by the story of the Tasaday.
   - ☐ c. only Manuel Elizalde knew that the Tasaday were fakes.

3. The author tells this story mainly by
   - ☐ a. comparing different topics.
   - ☐ b. telling different stories about the same topic.
   - ☐ c. telling about events in the order they happened.

F. Evaluate and Create

Put an X in the box next to the answer.

1. From what happened in the article, you can predict that if anyone else ever reports having found a Stone Age tribe,
   - ☐ a. scientists will ignore the news.
   - ☐ b. no one will believe the story.
   - ☐ c. scientists and reporters will check the facts more carefully.

2. What was the effect on the Tasaday of the crumbling of the Philippine government?
   - ☐ a. Elizalde began to persuade the Tasaday to talk to reporters.
   - ☐ b. The Tasaday started wearing modern clothes.
   - ☐ c. The Tasaday could no longer be hidden from the public.

3. Of the following themes, which one fits this story best?
   - ☐ a. It is impossible to keep up a lie, even for a short time.
   - ☐ b. Get proof before you believe an unusual story.
   - ☐ c. No one profits from a lie.

Unit 1 · Lesson 1.4

Near Death on the Football Field

Detroit Lions linebacker Reggie Brown lies motionless on the field after suffering a serious accident during a game in 1997.

Previewing the lesson gives you an idea of what you are going to read. To preview the lesson:

- look at the photograph and read the title and the photo caption.
- skim the article quickly to get a general idea of what it is about.
- read the questions after the article.

Before You Read
Preview

1   It would be the last game of the year for one team or the other. Would it be the New York Jets or the Detroit Lions? The winning team would go on to the National Football League playoffs. The losing team would be finished for the season. So there was a great deal at stake when the Jets and the Lions met in Detroit on December 21, 1997. Before the end of the day, though, there would be much more on the line than just a football game.

2   For three quarters, the game hung in the balance. Fans on both sides screamed and yelled on every play. Then all of a sudden the fans fell silent. They saw a player lying still on the field. It was Reggie Brown, a linebacker for the Lions. Brown had just tackled one of the Jets, but he had injured his spine when his helmet had hit the other man at a weird angle. As the rest of the players got up from the pile, Brown didn't move.

3   Luther Elliss, a Lion, offered his hand to help his teammate up. "Let's go," he said.

4   Brown still didn't react. He didn't move. "He just kind of mouthed the words, 'I can't get up,'" said Elliss.

5   Lions' trainer Kent Falb rushed onto the field. Kneeling by Brown's side, he saw right away that Brown was in trouble. "Dear God," he mumbled. "Don't let me lose another one." For a moment, Falb's mind flashed back to 1971. He had been on the field

Lesson 1.4 · Near Death on the Football Field   27

when Detroit Lion Chuck Hughes had died from a heart attack. Falb had also been there in 1991 when Lion Mike Utley had hurt his spine. Utley was never able to walk again.

6   Team doctor Terry Lock ran onto the field to join Falb. By this time Brown wasn't even breathing. His lips were turning blue. He had no pulse. To Falb and Lock it looked like a spinal injury. They knew they had to do something and do it fast.

7   Players on both sides crowded around. They, too, realized that Brown had suffered a serious injury. Some had tears in their eyes. Others went down on their knees to pray. Some of the players cried out for help. Lion Herman Moore couldn't bear to look. "It is a situation that you know can happen, but you don't believe it will," Moore said. "It seemed unreal. We take for granted when we hit the ground we're going to get back up."

8   The game was being broadcast on national TV, so millions of fans at home also saw Brown go down. One viewer was his mother. She usually didn't worry about her son getting hurt. So when the announcer said it was Brown on the field, she thought, "No, that can't be Reggie. There must be some mistake." Then she realized it was indeed her son lying there **immobile**. "I just dropped to my knees," she said, "and started praying."

immobile
still

9   Without breathing, Brown had only a few minutes to live. In most cases, doctors are careful not to move the neck of a person who has hurt his spine, but Falb and Lock felt they had no choice. They had to get Brown's helmet off. That was the only way they could begin mouth-to-mouth resuscitation. Falb lifted Brown's head and put his hand behind his neck. One

false move and Brown would die in his arms. Gently Lock slipped off the helmet.

10   Then Lock began to blow air into Brown's lungs. It worked. Brown's chest began to go up and down again. Soon he began breathing on his own. His pulse also came back. For the moment, at least, he was alive.

11   Carefully Brown was put on a special board to **support** his neck. By that time, he had been lying on the field for 17 minutes. To those who saw it, it seemed more like 17 hours. At last an ambulance came and took Brown to the hospital. Falb and Lock had done their best, but would it be enough? It looked like Brown would survive, but would he, like Utley, be unable to walk again?

support
hold up

12   The odds of a full recovery were not good. Doctors say that half of all people with this type of spinal cord injury never walk again. The 23-year-old Brown was lucky, though. Except for the injury, he was a strong, healthy young man. He was helped by the quick work of trainer Kent Falb and doctor Terry Lock. In addition, the doctors were able to use a brand new treatment on Brown. Six months earlier this treatment would not have been available.

13   Brown had a powerful **drive** to get well. From the start, he was determined to walk again. He had a lot of people pulling for him. Herman Moore showed him a video. It was filled with get-well messages from the Detroit Lions. Brown also got a letter from Mike Utley. It read: "Dear Reggie: Don't give up. Don't ever quit."

drive
desire

14   Reggie didn't quit. Soon he was back on his feet. He was shaky at first, but he got stronger with each day. Doctors didn't want him to move his neck or head for three months, so he wore a brace called a "halo" on his head. He wasn't as strong as he had been. His arms

recovered
got better

and feet often felt a bit numb. Still his doctors couldn't believe how fast he **recovered**. "I've never seen anyone else come so far so fast," said one.

blacked out
passed out

15 Brown considered himself a lucky man. He was later asked what he felt just before he **blacked out** on the field. Brown said that he thought for sure he was going to die. "I was thinking, 'I'm too young. I never had the chance to get married. I never had the chance to have kids. I never did this, I never did that.' It is a strange feeling when you know you are going to die."

16 Reggie Brown will never play football again. He can't do things that might hurt his head or neck, but he can do everything else. After leaving the hospital, he was asked about what he would do. "I want to do a lot of things," he said. "I'll never play football again. I'm sorry about that. This is just God's way of sending me down another avenue in life."

Timed Reading

If you have been timed while reading this article, enter your reading time below. Then turn to the Words-per-Minute table on page 121 and look up your reading speed (words per minute). Enter your reading speed on the graph on page 122.

Reading Time: Lesson 1.4

_____ : _____
Minutes   Seconds

COMPREHENSION & CRITICAL THINKING SKILLS

A Recognize and Recall Details

Put an X in the box next to the answer that correctly completes each statement about the article.

1. Reggie Brown was injured
   - ☐ a. when another player hit him at a weird angle.
   - ☐ b. while tackling one of the Jets.
   - ☐ c. while playing against the Detroit Lions.

2. When team doctor Terry Lock rushed onto the field,
   - ☐ a. he had tears in his eyes.
   - ☐ b. Brown wasn't even breathing.
   - ☐ c. Brown was having a heart attack.

3. Falb and Lock moved Brown's neck because
   - ☐ a. it was the only way they could remove his helmet and give him mouth-to-mouth resuscitation.
   - ☐ b. immediate neck movement helps heal a spinal injury.
   - ☐ c. they did not have time to wait for the ambulance to arrive.

4. A new treatment for spinal cord injuries
   - ☐ a. became available six months after Brown's injury.
   - ☐ b. helped Brown to recover quickly.
   - ☐ c. made Brown's hands and feet numb.

B Find the Main Idea

One of the statements below expresses the main idea of the article. One statement is too broad. The other statement is too narrow—it explains only part of the article. Label the statements using the following key:

M Main Idea	**B** Too Broad	**N** Too Narrow

____ 1. No one thought that Reggie Brown would walk again after being injured on the football field, but he surprised everyone with his quick recovery.

____ 2. According to doctors, half of the people with a spinal cord injury like Reggie Brown's never walk again.

____ 3. Many football players suffer serious injuries.

C Summarize and Paraphrase

1. Summarize paragraphs 9 and 10 in one or two sentences.
   _____
   _____
   _____
   _____

2. Put an X in the box next to the choice that completes the following summary of the article:

   The article about Reggie Brown begins with a description of how he was hurt and goes on to explain
   - ☐ **a.** how he recovered and continued to play football.
   - ☐ **b.** his treatment and recovery.
   - ☐ **c.** other injuries he had as a teenager.

3. Choose the sentence that correctly restates the following sentence from the article: "The odds of a full recovery are not good."
   - ☐ **a.** Recovery is impossible.
   - ☐ **b.** A full recovery is not a good thing.
   - ☐ **c.** The chances of recovering completely are low.

D Make Inferences

When you combine your own experience with information from a text to draw a conclusion that is not directly stated in the text, you are making an inference. The following inferences about the article may or may not be correct. Label the statements using the following key:

C Correct Inference	**F** Faulty Inference

____ 1. The absence of a pulse always means that a person has a serious spinal cord injury.

____ 2. It is extremely dangerous to move the neck of someone with a spinal cord injury.

____ 3. A spinal cord injury can affect a person's ability to walk.

____ 4. Reggie Brown could now become a soccer player.

____ 5. The support Brown received from friends and family helped him to recover more quickly.

E Recognize Author's Effect and Intentions

Put an X in the box next to the answer.

1. The main purpose of the first paragraph is to
   - ☐ a. describe the setting of the story.
   - ☐ b. describe the National Football League.
   - ☐ c. introduce Reggie Brown.

2. What does the author mean by the statement, "Before the end of the day, though, there would be much more on the line than just a football game"?
   - ☐ a. Before the end of the day, the football players would be lined up on the field.
   - ☐ b. Before the end of the day, something more important than the outcome of a football game would have happened.
   - ☐ c. Before the end of the day, the football game would be over and the players would leave.

3. The author probably wrote this article to
   - ☐ a. make people aware of the dangers of playing football.
   - ☐ b. tell Reggie Brown's inspiring story.
   - ☐ c. inform people about spinal injuries.

F Evaluate and Create

Put an X in the box next to the answer.

1. Which sentence gives an opinion?
   - ☐ a. Reggie Brown will never play football again.
   - ☐ b. Reggie Brown's chest began to go up and down again.
   - ☐ c. Reggie Brown is a lucky man.

2. From the information in the article, you can predict that Reggie Brown will
   - ☐ a. live a relatively normal life.
   - ☐ b. have difficulty walking.
   - ☐ c. become a football coach.

3. Which paragraph best supports your answer to question 2?
   - ☐ a. paragraph 12
   - ☐ b. paragraph 14
   - ☐ c. paragraph 16

Unit 1 · Lesson 1.5

The Mysterious Life of Twins

Paula Bernstein, left, and Elyse Schein, right, are identical twins who were separated at birth and reunited 35 years later. Scientists have been comparing the relationship between twins who grew up together and those who were separated at birth.

Making a connection between what you already know and what you read makes understanding new material easier. Ask yourself:

- Do I know any twins?
- How are these twins alike? How are they different?

Before You Read
Use Prior Knowledge

1 Jim Lewis was an identical twin, but he hadn't seen his brother since birth. The two boys were adopted by different families. They knew nothing about each other. Yet when they were brought together in 1979 after 39 years, something spooky seemed to be going on. For one thing, both boys had been named James. Both went by the nickname "Jim." As children, they both had a pet dog named Toy.

2 That was only the beginning. Each Jim had married a woman named Linda. Each then had a son. One named his son James Alan. The other named his son James Allan. Later, both Jims got divorced. Each had remarried—and in both cases, the second wife's name was Betty! Each Jim drove the same kind of blue car. Each had the same favorite drink. Each bit his nails, liked woodworking, and took vacations to the very same beach in Florida!

3 Could all of this be **coincidence** or do twins share a special connection? Scientists have long known that identical twins have the same genes. However, no one believed there was a gene that tells you what kind of car to buy. What made the "Jim" twins live such similar lives?

coincidence
chance event

4 In the past, people thought twins were alike simply because they grew up together. They saw the same people. They learned to like the same things. That is not the case with the "Jim" twins. They did not grow up together. They knew nothing about each other when they bought cars, named their sons, and picked out beaches.

Lesson 1.5 · The Mysterious Life of Twins

5   In the 1980s a man named Thomas J. Bouchard, Jr., took a closer look at twins. He found other sets of identical twins who had lived apart since birth. Among them were Daphne Goodship and Barbara Hebert. Like the "Jim" twins, these women had not seen each other for 39 years. Bouchard arranged for them to meet in London, England. At that meeting, Daphne and Barbara showed up wearing the same kind of clothes! Both had chosen a light brown dress and brown velvet jacket.

6   As the two women compared notes, they found they were alike in many ways. Both had the **weird** habit of pushing up their noses. Both had met their husbands at local dances when they were 16. Each of them had given birth to two sons and then a daughter. Strangest of all, each had fallen down the stairs at the age of 15. These accidents had left both twins with weak ankles.

weird
odd

7   Then there was Jack Yufe and Oskar Stöhr. Bouchard brought them together when they were 47 years old. It turned out that both men had short, clipped mustaches. Both wore rectangular, wire-rimmed glasses. Both showed up at their first meeting wearing the same kind of fancy blue shirt. Jack and Oskar soon found more "coincidences." They walked with the same kind of swinging steps. They shared the habit of keeping extra rubber bands around their wrists. Both of them read magazines from back to front. They both even had the odd habit of flushing a toilet before using it!

8   The twins in Bouchard's study were more alike than anyone would have guessed. None of them had been in touch with his or her twin growing up. So what led them to make so many of the same choices in life? Some people think twins can **communicate** with each other in mysterious ways. Ron and Rod Fuller are identical twins from Dallas, Texas. They say each can tell when the other one is in trouble.

communicate
make things known

Explains Rod, "There is a certain **bond** that we have for one another that I think all twins have."

bond
link

9   Other twins agree. Andreina and Andreini McPherson grew up in Chino Hills, California. They say they, too, can each tell how the other is feeling. In fact, they claim, they can feel each other's pain. When one of them is hurt, the other one can feel the injury.

10 If that is true, then maybe twins raised apart can also communicate in special ways. Did the twins from Bouchard's study send each other messages for years without knowing it? Perhaps. It may be that the answer lies in the genes, after all. In 1988 Dr. David Teplica began to study twins. He took pictures of 6,000 pairs of identical twins. He found some **amazing** things. These twins had freckles in the same spots. They got gray hairs at the same time and in the same places on their heads. Their faces got the same wrinkles. They even got pimples on their noses on exactly the same day! To Dr. Teplica, there was just one way to explain all this. Genes had to be controlling these events.

amazing
incredible

11 It's hard to believe we are born with genes that control when and where we get pimples, but that may be the case. Thomas Bouchard says his work also points to the power of genes. He believes genes explain many of the "coincidences" among the twins he studied. So who knows? Maybe there really is a gene that tells us what kind of car to buy.

....

If you have been timed while reading this article, enter your reading time below. Then turn to the Words-per-Minute table on page 121 and look up your reading speed (words per minute). Enter your reading speed on the graph on page 122.

Timed Reading

Reading Time: Lesson 1.5   _____ : _____
                                  Minutes   Seconds

COMPREHENSION & CRITICAL THINKING SKILLS

A Recognize and Recall Details

Put an X in the box next to the answer that correctly completes each statement about the article.

1. Scientists have long known that identical twins
   - ☐ a. have the same genes.
   - ☐ b. live identical lives.
   - ☐ c. are always lifelong friends.

2. When twins Daphne and Barbara met for the first time, they both
   - ☐ a. were late for the meeting.
   - ☐ b. wore the same kind of clothes.
   - ☐ c. had the same haircut.

3. Rod Fuller, a twin from Texas, says all twins have
   - ☐ a. similar likes and dislikes.
   - ☐ b. curiosity about the world.
   - ☐ c. a certain bond for one another.

4. Andreina and Andreini McPherson claim that when one of them gets hurt, the other
   - ☐ a. gets hurt the same way on the next day.
   - ☐ b. calls her on the phone.
   - ☐ c. can feel the pain.

B Find the Main Idea

One statement below expresses the main idea of the article. One statement is too broad. The other statement explains only part of the article—it is too narrow. Label the statements using the following key:

| **M** Main Idea | **B** Too Broad | **N** Too Narrow |

____ 1. There seems to be a special connection between twins, perhaps one that is related to their shared genes.

____ 2. Jim Lewis and his twin brother lived surprisingly similar lives, from the names of their children to their choice of cars.

____ 3. The study of twins has led to some interesting discoveries.

C Summarize and Paraphrase

Put an X in the box next to the answer.

1. Choose the summary that says the most important things about the article.
   - ☐ **a.** The study of twins may reveal interesting facts about all of us, from what we wear to the kind of car we drive.
   - ☐ **b.** Although people used to think that twins were alike only because they grew up together, recent research suggests other reasons for the similarities.
   - ☐ **c.** Twins who have always lived apart sometimes are eerily similar. These similarities suggest that genes are responsible for what happens to our bodies and minds.

2. Choose the sentence that correctly restates the following sentence: "The Twins in Bouchard's study were more alike than anyone would have guessed."
   - ☐ **a.** No one would have predicted that the twins whom Bouchard studied would be so similar.
   - ☐ **b.** When they were children, the twins in Bouchard's study guessed that they would always be alike.
   - ☐ **c.** Bouchard himself guessed that the twins in his study would be amazingly similar.

D Make Inferences

The following inferences about the article may or may not be correct. Label the statements using the following key:

C Correct Inference	**F** Faulty Inference

_____ 1. Pairs of identical twins always have the same taste in clothes, food, cars, and children's names.

_____ 2. There is a good chance that an identical twin will look more like his or her twin than anyone else.

_____ 3. Separating identical twins at birth never has an effect on their closeness or friendship later in life.

_____ 4. If twins are separated at birth and do not have any contact for a long period of time, they will never look or act alike.

_____ 5. Genes have a powerful influence on the characteristics of people's bodies and minds.

E. Recognize Author's Effect and Intentions

Put an X in the box next to the answer.

1. What is the author's purpose in writing "The Mysterious Life of Twins"?
   - ☐ a. to convey a mood of suspense
   - ☐ b. to inform the reader about amazing similarities between twins and to suggest a reason for these similarities
   - ☐ c. to describe a situation in which people met family members after living apart for many years

2. Choose the statement you believe the author would agree with.
   - ☐ a. Twins often seem to be strongly connected to each other even if they have never lived together.
   - ☐ b. Genes may have nothing to do with the strange similarities between twins.
   - ☐ c. It is possible to explain all similarities between twins by coincidence alone.

F. Evaluate and Create

Put an X in the box next to the answer.

1. Which statement from the article is an opinion?
   - ☐ a. In 1988 Dr. David Teplica began to study twins.
   - ☐ b. At the meeting, Daphne and Barbara showed up wearing the same kind of clothes.
   - ☐ c. It is ridiculous to think there could be a gene that tells you what kind of car to buy.

2. From the article, you can predict that scientists will
   - ☐ a. stop doing research on twins.
   - ☐ b. continue to do research on twins.
   - ☐ c. show that the results of the research done on twins are not useful or even true.

3. If you were a scientist, how could you best use the information in the article to learn more about the effect of genes on human development?
   - ☐ a. I could use it to plan further studies on twins.
   - ☐ b. I could use it to argue that doctors should separate all sets of twins at birth so that scientists can study them.
   - ☐ c. I could use it to prove without a doubt that identical twins do not have the same genes.

Unit 2 · Lesson 2.1

Mummies

Ancient Egyptians believed that when people died, they needed their bodies in the afterlife. The bodies were given a special treatment to keep them from decaying. These preserved bodies are called mummies. This Egyptian mummy dates from the 21st Dynasty (1070–945 B.C.).

Before You Read
Ask Questions

Look at the photograph on page 41 and read the photo caption. In a notebook, write several questions about mummies that you expect to be answered in the article.

Mummies

1   Have you ever considered dressing up as a mummy for Halloween? You could probably create a costume by wrapping yourself in a bunch of white bandages, but making a real mummy is not so easy. First, you need a dead body, and second, you need someone who understands the ancient art of mummy making.

2   A mummy is not the same as a skeleton. A skeleton is just bones, but a mummy has bones and skin. Often it has hair, fingernails, and muscles. Usually, these softer body parts **decay** quickly, but that doesn't happen with mummies. If a mummy has been properly prepared, it can last a long, long time.

decay
rot

3   Ancient Egyptians were master mummy makers. Some of their mummies are now more than 3,000 years old. These bodies still have lips, noses, ears, eyelids, and toenails. One has red hair and another's face remains twisted in a scream of death made thousands of years ago.

4   How did the Egyptians make such great mummies? Their secret was to dry each body **thoroughly**. If a body is totally dry, the flesh won't rot away. Drying a body means getting rid of all the fluids in it. To do this, Egyptians slit open the side of each body and scooped out much of the insides. They took out the stomach. They removed the liver, intestines, and lungs, but they did not remove the

thoroughly
completely

heart. The Egyptians believed the heart was the center of wisdom and truth, so they left it alone.

5   The brain was removed through the nose. Mummy makers stuck a long metal hook up the nose of the body. They scrambled the brain and partially liquefied it. Then they stored it and the other organs in jars.

6   Once Egyptians had cleaned out a body, they washed it with wine, packed it with a special salt called natron, and then they sat back and waited for 40 days. During that time, the natron soaked up liquid from the body. By the end of the 40 days, no liquid remained.

7   The drying-out process left bodies as **shriveled** as prunes, but Egyptians had a solution for that problem too. They stuffed the bodies with cloth or sand. That puffed the skin back up. Sometimes they put peppercorns up the nose. That helped push the nose back to its original shape. Egyptians also rubbed spices and herbs on the body to mask the smell of death.

shriveled shrunken and wrinkled

8   Next, mummy makers coated the dried body with a glue called resin. As the resin dried, it became hard. It formed a tough coating that protected the body and made it waterproof.

9   Finally, Egyptians wrapped each body in 20 layers, approximately 150 yards, of cloth. This was a difficult task that took several days. Sometimes an ear or toe fell off during the wrapping, but by the time the last layer was put on, the mummy was close to normal size again.

10   From 2600 B.C. to A.D. 300, Egyptians made millions of mummies. Almost everyone in Egypt who could afford it became one. Egyptians also mummified

animals. They turned cats, dogs, fish, snakes, birds, and even grasshoppers and beetles into mummies.

11   There was a reason for this "mummy mania." Egyptians believed living things needed their bodies after death. They believed dead people went on to the land of the gods. Even dead animals moved on to an **"afterlife."** Spirits of the dead could make contact with the gods, but those spirits needed a place to rest at night. They needed to return to their bodies. If their bodies had rotted away, the spirits would have no place to rest. Then the spirits, too, would die.

afterlife
life after death

12   Ancient Egyptians were not the only ones who believed in an afterlife. They weren't the only ones who made mummies, either. Halfway across the world, in the mountains of South America, people did the same thing. By 300 B.C., people in Peru and Chile had figured out a method to **preserve** dead bodies. They did not dry them with salt. Instead, they set them out in the hot sun or put them over a fire. The heat and smoke helped to remove all of the liquids from the body. Once the bodies were dry, they were wrapped up and put in baskets. In Egypt, mummies were stretched out flat. However, most South American mummies had their knees folded up to their chins.

preserve
keep safe from decay

13   Not all mummies are thousands of years old. About 400 years ago, some people in Italy started making mummies. They felt it would help them keep in touch with the spirits of those who had died. These Italians put the bodies in a special room. They left them there for a year. During that time, all fluids drained out of the bodies. Then the bodies were laid in the sun. When they were fully dried, they were dressed in fancy clothes and placed in underground rooms called catacombs.

14   People often visited the mummies in the catacombs. They brought picnic lunches to eat, talked to the mummies, asked them for advice, and even held hands with the mummies as they said prayers.

15   The last Italian mummy was created in 1920. It was made from the body of a little girl named Rosalia Lombardo. Rosalia died at the age of two. Her father took her body to a man named Alfredo Salafia, who knew how to mummify dead bodies. In fact, Salafia had developed a new system for it, and he used this system on little Rosalia. The results were amazing. Rosalia's body was perfectly preserved for many years. It was not shriveled at all. In fact, it looked as though Rosalia was just taking a nap.

16   For several years, no one knew what Salafia's system was. He died before sharing it with the world, but his technique was recently discovered in a handwritten memoir.

17   Some people think mummies are a good way to honor the dead, but others don't even like to look at them. You might want to keep that in mind if you ever do dress up like a mummy for Halloween.

If you have been timed while reading this article, enter your reading time below. Then turn to the Words-per-Minute table on page 121 and look up your reading speed (words per minute). Enter your reading speed on the graph on page 122.

Timed Reading

Reading Time: Lesson 2.1

_____ : _____

Minutes   Seconds

COMPREHENSION & CRITICAL THINKING SKILLS

A Recognize and Recall Details

Put an X in the box next to the answer that correctly completes each statement about the article.

1. For the ancient Egyptians, the first step in making a mummy was to
   - ☐ a. put the body out in the sun.
   - ☐ b. remove most of the inner organs and the brain.
   - ☐ c. wrap the body in layers of cloth.
2. The Egyptians thought that, at death, the spirit
   - ☐ a. died along with its body.
   - ☐ b. left the body forever to go to the gods.
   - ☐ c. visited the gods but returned to its body to rest.
3. Usually, mummies made in South America
   - ☐ a. were dressed in fancy clothes.
   - ☐ b. had their knees folded up to their chins.
   - ☐ c. were buried in large wooden boxes.
4. Italians who made mummies during the last 400 years did so in order to
   - ☐ a. keep in touch with the spirits of the dead.
   - ☐ b. display the mummies in museums.
   - ☐ c. save the bodies of the dead for future cures.

B Find the Main Idea

One of the statements below expresses the main idea of the article. One statement is too broad. The other statement is too narrow—it explains only part of the article. Label the statements using the following key:

M Main Idea	B Too Broad	N Too Narrow

____ 1. Many people around the world and in different times shared a belief in the afterlife, and this belief affected burial customs.

____ 2. The Egyptians used a detailed mummy-making process that involved drying and treating dead bodies. People from other areas of the world have made mummies as well, using a similar process.

____ 3. Many mummies have bones, skin, hair, fingernails, and muscles.

C Summarize and Paraphrase

Put an X in the box next to the answer.

1. Choose the summary that says all the most important things about the article in the fewest words.

    ☐ **a.** Ancient Egyptians are famous for their skill in making mummies. In their process, most of the body's internal organs were taken out and the body was dried out completely.

    ☐ **b.** For thousands of years, people around the world preserved dead bodies as mummies. First the body was emptied of liquid and then it was dried out completely. Different cultures completed the drying-out process in different ways.

    ☐ **c.** Mummies in Egypt were laid out flat in their coffins, but most mummies of South America were arranged with their knees folded up to their chins. Italian mummies were dressed in fancy clothes.

2. From the following one-sentence summaries, choose the best description of the article.

    ☐ **a.** In the past, Egyptians and others preserved dead bodies as mummies.

    ☐ **b.** Egyptians made mummies for more than 2,000 years.

    ☐ **c.** In South America, people dried dead bodies over a fire.

3. Choose the sentence that correctly restates the following sentence from the article: "Once Egyptians had cleaned out a body, they washed it with wine."

    ☐ **a.** Egyptians washed the body with wine after cleaning it out.

    ☐ **b.** After washing it with wine, the Egyptians cleaned out the body.

    ☐ **c.** Egyptians cleaned the body with wine and then washed it thoroughly.

D Make Inferences

The following inferences about the article may or may not be correct. Label the statements using the following key:

C Correct Inference	**F** Faulty Inference

_____ **1.** In ancient Egypt, making a mummy was an expensive procedure.

_____ **2.** Making mummies is easier in desert areas than in rainy lands.

_____ **3.** People in South America learned to make mummies from Egyptians.

_____ **4.** Ancient Egyptians might think that a Halloween mummy costume shows disrespect for the dead.

E Recognize Author's Effect and Intentions

Put an **X** in the box next to the answer.

1. What does the author of the article imply by stating, "Egyptians also mummified animals"?
   - ☐ **a.** Egyptians thought that animals had spirits, and that the spirits would need their bodies after death.
   - ☐ **b.** Egyptians thought that animal mummies would make nice decorations for the tombs of their loved ones.
   - ☐ **c.** Egyptians who made mummies worked on animals when they had nothing else to do.

2. The author probably wrote this article to
   - ☐ **a.** inform the reader about the history of mummy making and some of the processes involved.
   - ☐ **b.** inform the reader about people who try to mummify dead bodies in scientific laboratories today.
   - ☐ **c.** point out the difference between beliefs of people in ancient times and beliefs of people today.

F Evaluate and Create

Put an **X** in the box next to the answer.

1. Which of the following statements is an opinion rather than a fact?
   - ☐ **a.** From 2600 B.C. to A.D. 300, Egyptians made millions of mummies.
   - ☐ **b.** The last Italian mummy was created in 1920.
   - ☐ **c.** The process of making mummies is more amazing than modern technology.

2. If you were a taxidermist (someone who stuffs and mounts dead animals), what is one way in which your job would be similar to the process of mummy making as discussed in the article?
   - ☐ **a.** Like the Italians, I would dress the animals up in fancy clothes after leaving them in a room for a year.
   - ☐ **b.** My first step would be the same; I would make sure to dry the bodies completely.
   - ☐ **c.** I would weigh the bodies to determine how much liquid I would need to dry up.

Unit 2 · Lesson 2.2

Escape from Iran

In mid-January of 1980, the Canadian ambassador to Iran, Ken Taylor, briefed reporters on the status of the American hostage crisis in Tehran. On January 28, 1980, he left the country with the six Americans whom he had rescued. Taylor later revealed that he was working for the CIA at the time.

Before You Read
Clarify

You may not understand a word the first time you see it, such as *embassy* in the first paragraph of the article. To clarify the meaning, ask yourself, "Does the word look like other words I know?" You may also use a dictionary to find the meaning.

Escape from Iran

1   It came as a total shock. No one is ever supposed to attack the embassy of another country, but that is what happened late in the morning of November 4, 1979. A mob of people filled the streets in Tehran, the capital city of Iran. They stormed the U.S. Embassy. They climbed over the walls, waved guns in the air, and shouted, "Death to America!"

2   In just a few minutes, the Iranians took control of the embassy. They captured 52 Americans and held them prisoner for the next 444 days. But six Americans escaped the mob. They slipped out a back door. They ran into the street. They didn't know which way to turn. All they knew was that they were not safe. If anyone saw them, they would be taken **hostage** or possibly killed.

hostage
prisoner

3   Desperate, the six men and women went to the Canadian Embassy. They asked the Canadians to hide them. It wasn't a simple favor. If the Canadians agreed, they would be risking their own lives. The Iranians might find out and attack the Canadians.

4   Canada's Ambassador, Ken Taylor, knew that, so he gathered his staff and informed them about the danger. Then he asked them what he should do. The Canadians didn't flinch. They wanted to help. Some even offered to hide Americans in their own homes. Taylor and his wife did this. They hid Joseph and Kathy Stafford.

5   Taylor's staff hoped to smuggle the six Americans out of Iran to safety. But how? The airports and train

stations were closely watched. Any American trying to leave would be immediately arrested. So Taylor watched and waited. He sent some of his staff out of the country on unnecessary trips in order to find out how hard it would be to sneak someone out of Iran. He also wanted airport officials in Iran to get used to Canadians going in and out of the country.

6   Meanwhile, back in the United States, Antonio Mendez learned about the six men and women. Mendez worked for the CIA, America's spy agency. Mendez went to work on his own scheme for helping the six Americans. He talked to officials in Canada and got them to issue six fake Canadian passports. The Americans would need these if they had any hope of slipping out of Iran undetected.

7   Then Mendez dreamed up a bold plan. It was like something out of a movie. Mendez pretended to be an Irish filmmaker. In order to convince Iranians that he really was making a film, he opened an office for his **phony** company, and even hired people to work for it. Mendez decided his bogus film would be a science-fiction thriller called *Argo*. He created a script that called for some scenes to be shot in Tehran.

phony
fake

8   During this time, things remained **tense** for the six Americans and their Canadian hosts. All of them were afraid their secret would be discovered. On January 19, 1980, their fears were realized. On that day Taylor's wife, Patricia, got a phone call.

tense
stressful

9   "May I speak to Mr. or Mrs. Stafford?" the caller asked.

10   The question shook Patricia. No one knew that Joseph and Kathy Stafford were hiding in her house.

11   "I'm sorry," she said, trying to sound calm. "There is no one by that name living here."

12   The caller repeated his question. He said he knew that the Staffords were there. At last, Patricia hung up.

13   The six Americans were now in even greater danger. They would have to get out of Iran, and they would have to move swiftly. The Canadians would have to clear out too. The Iranians might attack them for helping the Americans. Over the next few days, Taylor sent several of his staff members on trips out of Iran. None of them returned. Soon he had only four staff members left at the embassy.

14   At that point, Antonio Mendez arrived. He had entered Iran without any trouble. After all, his phony passport showed that he was Irish, not American. Mendez told Iranian officials he had come to work on his film, but he told Taylor the truth. He had come to help get the six Americans out of the country.

15   Taylor arranged for Mendez and the Americans to get together. Mendez gave them the fake Canadian passports. He told them they were going to pose as members of his fake film company. Kathleen Stafford, for instance, would be the *Argo* set designer, and Cora Lijek would be a screenwriter.

16   Mendez helped the Americans dress for their parts. He had Mark Lijek dye his beard black. He gave Kathleen Stafford a thick pair of glasses to wear. Bob Anders usually dressed in dark suits, but Mendez had him put on tight pants and a blue silk shirt that was open at the top. Mendez also puffed up Anders's hair into a big wave and then he put a **flashy** gold chain around his neck.

flashy
shiny

17   On January 28, the Americans went to the airport. Disguised as part of the *Argo* crew, they headed for a flight out of the country. As Mendez held his breath, they flashed their Canadian passports. The Iranians never gave them a second look. They all got on a

plane for Germany and freedom. The same day, Taylor and his three remaining staff members quietly flew to Europe also.

18   It took the Iranians a while to figure out what had occurred, but when they did, they were furious. Their **outrage** was aimed at the Canadians, and they branded Taylor and his staff outlaws. They even issued threats against Canada. A spokesman for Iran declared, "Sooner or later, somewhere in the world, Canada will pay for this crime."

outrage
anger

19   To Americans, though, the Canadians were heroes. Taylor and his staff had risked their lives to help six frightened souls get out of Iran. Americans flooded the Canadian government with thank-you cards. They flew Canadian flags next to American ones, and all across the United States, people put up big signs that said, "Thank You, Canada."

20   Antonio Mendez had sworn an oath of secrecy, so no one knew what role he had played. No one stopped to shake his hand in the street. He got no signs or thank-you notes, and that was just fine with him. From his point of view, his daring actions had just been part of the job. It was years before the world found out that the CIA had also taken part in the rescue. Ken Taylor revealed in January 2010 that he worked as a CIA spy during the 1979 hostage crisis.

If you have been timed while reading this article, enter your reading time below. Then turn to the Words-per-Minute table on page 121 and look up your reading speed (words per minute). Enter your reading speed on the graph on page 122.

Timed Reading

Reading Time: Lesson 2.2

_____ : _____

Minutes   Seconds

COMPREHENSION & CRITICAL THINKING SKILLS

A Recognize and Recall Details

Put an **X** in the box next to the answer that correctly completes each statement about the article.

1. When the Iranians attacked the U.S. Embassy,
   - ☐ **a.** they took 444 people prisoner.
   - ☐ **b.** they killed 52 Americans.
   - ☐ **c.** six Americans escaped.
2. When Antonio Mendez of the CIA learned that the six Americans were in hiding, he
   - ☐ **a.** issued them fake German passports.
   - ☐ **b.** came up with a plan to help them escape by having them pose as members of a fake film company.
   - ☐ **c.** filmed an entire science fiction film in Tehran that was called *Argo*.
3. No one knew that the CIA helped with the escape because Mendez
   - ☐ **a.** was not supposed to help.
   - ☐ **b.** did not want to be considered a hero.
   - ☐ **c.** had sworn an oath of secrecy.

B Find the Main Idea

One of the statements below expresses the main idea of the article. One statement is too broad. The other statement is too narrow—it explains only part of the article. Label the statements using the following key:

M Main Idea	**B** Too Broad	**N** Too Narrow

_____ 1. To escape from Iran, a group of Americans pretended to be members of a fake film company.

_____ 2. The Canadian government helped U.S. citizens in 1979 when the U.S. Embassy was attacked.

_____ 3. When the U.S. Embassy in Tehran, Iran, was attacked, Canada's ambassador sheltered six Americans who had escaped the embassy and helped them get out of the country.

C Summarize and Paraphrase

1. Look for the important ideas and events in paragraphs 2 and 3. Summarize these paragraphs in no more than 25 words.

   _____
   _____
   _____
   _____

   Now shorten your summary to 15 words or less without leaving out any essential information.

   _____
   _____
   _____

2. Read the statement below. Then read the paraphrase of that statement. Choose the sentence that best tells why the paraphrase does not say the same thing as the statement.

   Statement: It took the Iranians a while to figure out what had occurred.

   Paraphrase: The Iranians knew immediately what had occurred.

   ☐ **a.** The paraphrase says too much.
   ☐ **b.** The paraphrase doesn't say enough.
   ☐ **c.** The paraphrase doesn't match the statement.

D Make Inferences

The following inferences about the article may or may not be correct. Label the statements using the following key:

C Correct Inference	**F** Faulty Inference

____ 1. In 1979 many Iranians did not like America.
____ 2. The Canadian Embassy in Tehran is near the American Embassy.
____ 3. All of the people taken hostage in the embassy attack were killed.
____ 4. Antonio Mendez had helped people escape from hostile countries before.
____ 5. Members of the CIA are not allowed to talk about their work to people outside the organization.

E Recognize Author's Effect and Intentions

Put an **X** in the box next to the answer.

1. What is the author's purpose in writing "Escape from Iran"?
   - ☐ **a.** to convey the Iranians' feelings of frustration and anger towards the United States in 1979
   - ☐ **b.** to describe how Ken Taylor and Antonio Mendez helped six Americans escape from Iran
   - ☐ **c.** to express an opinion about the Iranians' actions

2. From the statements below, choose the one that you believe the author would agree with.
   - ☐ **a.** The efforts of Ken Taylor and Antonio Mendez to help the six Americans were heroic.
   - ☐ **b.** The Canadians should not have helped the Americans.
   - ☐ **c.** The CIA should not have gotten involved in the situation.

F Evaluate and Create

Put an **X** in the box next to the answer.

1. Which of the following sentences expresses an opinion?
   - ☐ **a.** The Iranians had no good reason to be angry with America or to attack the U.S. embassy.
   - ☐ **b.** A group of Iranians attacked the U.S. Embassy on November 4, 1979, and captured 52 Americans.
   - ☐ **c.** Mendez told Iranian officials he had come to work on his science-fiction film.

2. The six Americans were relieved when they escaped the embassy, but
   - ☐ **a.** they didn't know where to go.
   - ☐ **b.** they did not want to dress like Canadians.
   - ☐ **c.** they were lost.

3. According to paragraph 6, Antonio Mendez got fake Canadian passports for the Americans because
   - ☐ **a.** he wanted them to work on his film.
   - ☐ **b.** he worked for the CIA.
   - ☐ **c.** they would need them to get out of Iran.

Unit 2 · Lesson 2.3

Alone at Sea

Dr. Alain Bombard crossed the Atlantic Ocean in this 15-foot raft. He survived for weeks on raw fish, plankton, and seawater. He proved that people can stay alive without fresh water for longer than 10 days, the previously determined limit.

Before You Read
Predict

Look at the photograph on page 57 and read the title and photo caption. Predict what will happen. How will Dr. Bombard survive a long trip on the ocean while drinking only salt water?

....

🔊 Alone at Sea

1 Suppose you are lost at sea. You're floating on a raft in the middle of the ocean with no fresh water to drink. What should you do? Should you drink from the sea? If you do, will you go mad? Will you die a terrible, agonizing death?

2 Over the years many sailors have been lost at sea. Most of them have refused to drink the salt water that was all around them. They believed they would die if they did. They thought drinking water from the ocean would drive them crazy with thirst and would **hasten** their deaths. Many knew of shipwrecked sailors who had, in desperation, consumed salt water. These men had been racked with terrible pains. They went out of their minds and finally died.

hasten
speed up

3 Because of such tales, most stranded sailors avoided drinking even small amounts of salt water. They just waited in misery while their bodies slowly became **dehydrated**. A human being can live 30 days without food, but a person can live only 10 days without water.

dehydrated
dry

4 Alain Bombard, a 27-year-old French doctor, wanted to save the lives of shipwrecked sailors. He felt it was a mistake for them not to drink seawater. In fact, he thought they should begin drinking it right away, before they became dehydrated. If they did that, he thought, their bodies could handle the extra salt. Then they could live much longer than 10 days.

5   To prove his point, Bombard decided to "shipwreck" himself. His plan was to drink a bit of seawater every day. Beyond that, he would get some water by squeezing the liquid out of fish he caught. Finally, he might pick up some rainwater here and there. Bombard was confident he could survive many days this way. When he told people about his plan, they thought he was out of his mind.

6   On May 25, 1952, Bombard started his test. He cast himself adrift in the Mediterranean Sea in a rubber boat. A sailor named Jack Palmer went with him. The test was a flop. "The winds and currents drove us in circles for days," Bombard said. Worse still, the Mediterranean Sea didn't contain many fish. Bombard and Palmer had trouble catching enough to stay alive. Still they survived more than two weeks. Drinking the salt water didn't make them crazy, but the voyage wasn't much fun.

7   Still Bombard wasn't ready to give up. In fact, he wanted to try floating his raft across the entire Atlantic Ocean. Jack Palmer, on the other hand, had seen enough. He thought it would be suicide to head out across the ocean without fresh water.

8   So on October 19, 1952, Bombard set out across the Atlantic alone. He sailed in a 15-foot rubber boat. It had a wooden floor and a small mast. If Bombard made it all the way to the West Indies, he would have proved his theory. If he died, at least he felt his death would be for a noble cause.

9   Bombard did carry some food and water with him. He could use them to save his life, but if he did, his voyage would be a failure. To make sure no one could later claim he cheated, Bombard had officials lock the supplies with a special seal. If the seal was broken, everyone would know his theory had failed.

10 Other than these emergency supplies, Bombard took no food and no water. His food and drink would have to come from the sea. On this journey, he had no problem finding food. "There were plenty of fish," Bombard said. "Little flying fish struck against my sail and fell in the raft." He also fished with a makeshift harpoon. Of course, he had no stove. So he ate the fish **raw**. The pink flesh didn't look very good, but he found that the taste wasn't bad.

raw
uncooked

11 Bombard knew he couldn't live just on fish. If he did, he would get scurvy, a disease that comes from not getting the right vitamins. So Bombard dragged a piece of cloth behind the boat to catch plankton. Eating these tiny sea organisms helped to balance his diet.

12 For liquid, Bombard drank one and a half pints of seawater each day. He also drank the juice he squeezed from fish. "For 23 days I had no rainwater, but fish juices served the purpose. I had no trouble with real thirst."

13 Bombard did, however, have trouble with loneliness. At times he was frightened by the "terror of the open sea." He longed for the sound of human voices. The only noises he heard during his journey were "the rushing of the wind, the watery hiss of the breaking waves, and the nervous flutter of the sail."

14 Early in his voyage, a storm almost destroyed his boat. Bombard had been sailing less than a week when the storm struck. Huge waves battered the boat. "One minute I perched atop the waves like a surfboard," he recalled, "the next, I was in a **hollow** so deep I could barely feel the wind." Strong winds ripped his sail. They also ruined his spare sail. Luckily, Bombard managed to sew the first sail back together.

hollow
hole

15   The next weeks passed quite uneventfully. Then, after about a month and a half, the wind suddenly died. Bombard's boat stopped moving. After several days of deadly calm, he began to fear he would never reach the West Indies. If he died now, nobody would know that he had survived so long.

16   Then, at last, a British ship appeared on the horizon. The ship's captain couldn't believe Bombard was still alive. By this time, the French doctor had been at sea for 53 days. Bombard was heartbroken to learn that he was still 600 miles from the West Indies. Still, he had proven his theory. According to the old belief, he should have died six weeks earlier.

17   Bombard could have ended his journey right then and there, but he wanted to continue on to the West Indies. So after a **meager** meal on board the ship, he climbed back into his boat. His spirits had been restored. Happily, the wind began to blow again.

meager
small

18   On December 23, 1952, Dr. Alain Bombard reached the West Indies. He had been at sea for 65 days. He had sailed more than 2,750 miles and had lost 56 pounds, but he was alive. He had proven his theory! Just in case someone doubted him, the seal on his emergency supplies was unbroken.

If you have been timed while reading this article, enter your reading time below. Then turn to the Words-per-Minute table on page 121 and look up your reading speed (words per minute). Enter your reading speed on the graph on page 122.

Timed Reading

Reading Time: Lesson 2.3

_____ : _____
Minutes   Seconds

COMPREHENSION & CRITICAL THINKING SKILLS

A Recognize and Recall Details

Put an X in the box next to the answer that correctly completes each statement about the article.

1. Many people believed that drinking salt water would
   - ☐ a. help a person to live 10 days.
   - ☐ b. cause a person to go crazy and die.
   - ☐ c. poison someone.

2. Dr. Alain Bombard believed that
   - ☐ a. drinking seawater was good for the body.
   - ☐ b. sailors should not drink seawater.
   - ☐ c. if people began drinking seawater before they became dehydrated, their bodies could handle the extra salt.

3. When Bombard sailed across the Atlantic Ocean,
   - ☐ a. he carried some food and water in a sealed container.
   - ☐ b. a sailor named Jack Palmer went with him.
   - ☐ c. he carried no extra food or water.

4. Bombard's biggest problem while he was at sea was
   - ☐ a. loneliness.
   - ☐ b. storms.
   - ☐ c. thirst.

B Find the Main Idea

One of the statements below expresses the main idea of the article. One statement is too broad. The other statement is too narrow—it explains only part of the article. Label the statements using the following key:

| **M** Main Idea | **B** Too Broad | **N** Too Narrow |

_____ 1. By surviving a trip across the Atlantic Ocean eating and drinking only what he found in the sea, Dr. Alain Bombard proved that it is possible to drink only salt water for long periods of time and stay alive.

_____ 2. Dr. Alain Bombard proved that people could drink salt water for weeks.

_____ 3. Dr. Alain Bombard's trip across the Atlantic Ocean lasted 65 days.

C Summarize and Paraphrase

Put an **X** in the box next to the answer.

1. Choose the summary that states the most important things about the article.
   - ☐ **a.** Dr. Alain Bombard believed that people could drink salt water and survive. He proved this by crossing the Atlantic Ocean in a raft, eating and drinking only what he could find at sea.
   - ☐ **b.** Alain Bombard survived 65 days at sea drinking only salt water and eating fish and plankton.
   - ☐ **c.** Dr. Alain Bombard "shipwrecked" himself twice, surviving only on what he could find in the sea. His second trip lasted 65 days.

2. Choose the best paraphrase for the following sentence: "At times he was frightened by the 'terror of the open sea.'"
   - ☐ **a.** Sometimes he was afraid because he could see nothing but the sea all around him.
   - ☐ **b.** Sometimes he was afraid of sharks, the terrors of the sea.
   - ☐ **c.** Sometimes he was afraid of drowning in the sea.

3. Choose the best paraphrase for this sentence: "And, just in case someone doubted him, the seal on his emergency supplies was unbroken."
   - ☐ **a.** Someone doubted that his emergency supplies had been opened.
   - ☐ **b.** Just in case his emergency supplies ran out, he broke the seal.
   - ☐ **c.** His emergency supplies were still sealed as proof to doubters.

D Make Inferences

When you combine your own experience with information from a text to draw a conclusion that is not directly stated in the text, you are making an inference. The following inferences about the article may or may not be correct. Label the statements using the following key:

C Correct Inference	**F** Faulty Inference

_____ **1.** People should drink salt water.

_____ **2.** Drinking salt water in small quantities is safe.

_____ **3.** Alain Bombard had never sailed before.

_____ **4.** Bombard's raft did not have a motor.

_____ **5.** Sailors crossing an ocean today usually drink salt water.

E Recognize Author's Effect and Intentions
Put an X in the box next to the answer.
1. The main purpose of the first paragraph is to
   - ☐ **a.** introduce the topic of the article.
   - ☐ **b.** describe what happens when a person drinks salt water.
   - ☐ **c.** inform the reader about salt water.
2. What is the author's purpose in writing "Alone at Sea"?
   - ☐ **a.** to express an opinion about Alain Bombard
   - ☐ **b.** to describe Alain Bombard's journey
   - ☐ **c.** to encourage the reader to drink salt water
3. Choose the statement that you believe the author would agree with.
   - ☐ **a.** People shouldn't go out to sea alone.
   - ☐ **b.** In an emergency, it is OK to drink salt water; but in general drinking salt water is not a good idea.
   - ☐ **c.** Alain Bombard's experiment is not very interesting.

F Evaluate and Create
1. List at least two ways in which Bombard's two "shipwrecks" were similar and two ways in which they were different.

   Similarities
   _____
   _____
   _____

   Differences
   _____
   _____
   _____

2. Which paragraph does not provide evidence from the article to support your answers to question 1?
   - ☐ **a.** paragraph 6
   - ☐ **b.** paragraph 10
   - ☐ **c.** paragraph 17

Unit 2 · Lesson 2.4

Night Killers

Like the mythical creature it was named for, the vampire bat drinks its victim's blood. The vampire bat usually ignores humans, preferring to drink the blood of large animals. If necessary, though, it will drink any blood it can find.

Before You Read
Make Connections

Read the title and photo caption and connect the information with things you have learned or experienced. Describe a story you have heard, a book you have read, or a movie or TV program you have seen that was about vampires or vampire bats.

Night Killers

1   They come out at night. Flying just three feet above the ground, they are constantly on the lookout for blood. Their four white fangs glisten in the light of the moon. They hunt by sound and by smell. As they swoop past, they make an angry sputtering noise. These night killers are vampire bats. You don't want to be around when they're out looking for a meal.

2   Vampire bats live in parts of Mexico, Central America, and South America. They are not very big. Most weigh only about one ounce. Their bodies are just three inches long, or the size of a human thumb. Even with their wings stretched out, they are only eight inches wide. Still, these tiny creatures can kill a cow. Just ask Cesar Murillo, a cattle rancher in Mexico. In 1995 vampire bats killed more than 50 cows in his herd. Using heat sensors in the nose, vampire bats find a vein close to the surface of the victim's skin. Legend says they suck the blood out of their victim. That isn't true, though. Instead, they use their sharp teeth to cut the flesh. Often they make their incision behind an ear or a hoof. Then they lick the blood from the open wound. Vampire bats can drink their own body weight in warm blood at one meal. That can take a while. Sometimes their **gory** feast will last as long as 20 minutes.

gory
bloody and horrible

3   Because vampire bats come out at night, their victims are usually asleep at the time of the attack. The bats have a special chemical in their saliva.

It numbs the victim's skin. That way, they can sink their teeth in without waking the victim. The bats use a second chemical to keep the blood from drying up while they eat.

4   The real trouble with these nasty creatures isn't the blood they take away. It's the diseases they leave behind. Vampire bats carry several deadly diseases, including rabies. That's how they killed Cesar Murillo's cows. As they lapped up the cows' blood, they infected the cows with rabies.

5   Within a few days, the cows began to act very strangely. Murillo described how the disease affects cows. "They start to lose their ability to walk," he said. "Their back legs buckle when they try to stand. Then they start trying to crawl. They get this desperate look in their eyes. A short time later, they die."

6   As bad as the situation was for Murillo, it was much worse for people in Nicaragua. There, in 1999, vampire bats started to attack humans. One morning, the parents of two young girls woke up to find vampire bats drinking the blood of their sleeping daughters. In another case, a small girl died from rabies after being attacked by vampire bats. In all, the bats attacked at least 22 people.

7   These attacks were most unusual. Vampire bats prefer the blood of large birds, cows, horses, and pigs. They live in deep caves or old wells. Normally they don't go near humans. In 1998 Hurricane Mitch struck Nicaragua. That storm brought record-breaking rains. Many caves and wells were flooded. Bats were forced out of their rural homes and into places where people lived. (Heavy rains had also helped **trigger** the outbreak of bat attacks on cows in Mexico.)

trigger
set off

8   In one Nicaraguan town, people had to fight the bats for several months. "Every night they're after us," said one farmer. "The cows, the horses, and us too."

9   Many people in the town rubbed garlic on their animals. Aris Mejia explained why. Mejia was one of a dozen bat killers hired by the government. "The bats just don't like the odor of garlic," he said. "It only lasts one night, however. If you don't put fresh garlic on the animals the next night, the bats come back."

permanent
lasting

slaying
killing

10   Mejia found a more **permanent** solution. His job was to kill as many vampire bats as he could. He started hunting each night as soon as the sun went down. **Slaying** bats wasn't a nice job. "It's kind of strange work, and not everyone in Nicaragua likes to do it," said Mejia. "You can always tell us by our scars." One vampire bat left an ugly scar on his left hand. It bit right through the thick gloves he was wearing.

11   Mejia didn't hunt vampire bats with a gun. He didn't try to expose them to the sunlight. He didn't try to drive a stake through their hearts. Those weapons are used only in fiction when the villain is a human vampire. Instead, Mejia went after the bats with a net. If he could find where they lived, he would cover the entrance with his net. He could then trap the bats when they tried to come out.

12   If he couldn't find the bats' homes, Mejia used a different approach. He would have a farmer put all his animals in one corral. In this way, the cows, horses, and pigs would serve as bait. Then Mejia would wait. He knew the vampire bats would find them in a few nights. When they did, he would be waiting for them with his net.

13   After catching a bat, Mejia would smear it with poison and then let it go. The poison was strong enough to kill the bat, but it acted slowly. That was the plan. The released bat would fly back to its home. Other bats in the colony would then lick the poisoned bat in an attempt to clean it. Or sometimes the bats would fight and bite the poisoned bat. Either way, the others would swallow the poison. Within a few days all the bats in that colony would be dead. "For every bat we capture," said Mejia, "we can kill up to 10 or 15."

14   To many people, poisoning vampire bats sounds cruel. After all, most of the time these tiny creatures are not a big threat. They stay away from humans and attack only a few farm animals. However, if heavy rains force the bats to look for food in other places, they become a huge problem. No one wants to wake up to find a vampire bat licking blood from his or her toes. When bats start to attack humans, bat killers such as Aris Mejia are **in big demand.**

in big demand
wanted badly

If you have been timed while reading this article, enter your reading time below. Then turn to the Words-per-Minute table on page 121 and look up your reading speed (words per minute). Enter your reading speed on the graph on page 122.

Timed Reading

Reading Time: Lesson 2.4

_____ : _____

Minutes   Seconds

COMPREHENSION & CRITICAL THINKING SKILLS

A Recognize and Recall Details

Put an X in the box next to the answer that correctly completes each statement about the article.

1. Vampire bats are about
   - ☐ a. eight inches from head to toe.
   - ☐ b. three inches from head to toe.
   - ☐ c. three inches from the tip of one wing to the tip of the other.
2. Victims don't wake up when vampire bats bite them because
   - ☐ a. the bats have a numbing chemical in their saliva.
   - ☐ b. the victims are already dead when the bats attack them.
   - ☐ c. the bats never break through the victims' skin.
3. The worst threat that vampire bats pose to humans is
   - ☐ a. a loss of blood.
   - ☐ b. the spread of diseases such as rabies.
   - ☐ c. the poisoning of farm animals.
4. Bats don't like the smell of
   - ☐ a. farm animals.
   - ☐ b. human blood.
   - ☐ c. garlic.

B Find the Main Idea

One of the statements below expresses the main idea of the article. One statement is too broad. The other statement is too narrow—it explains only part of the article. Label the statements using the following key:

M Main Idea	B Too Broad	N Too Narrow

____ 1. Vampire bats usually drink animal blood. When floods drive vampire bats to towns and farms, the bats can spread disease and cause death to both animals and humans.

____ 2. Vampire bats are not usually dangerous, but they can become deadly.

____ 3. Vampire bats attacked 22 people in Nicaragua in 1999, causing the death of at least one person.

C Summarize and Paraphrase

1. Reread paragraph 4 of the article. Below, write a summary of the paragraph in no more than 25 words.

   _____
   _____
   _____
   _____

   Now rewrite your summary in no more than 15 words.

   _____
   _____

2. Put an X next to the sentence that correctly restates this sentence from the article: "Because vampire bats come out at night, their victims are usually asleep at the time of the attack."

   ☐ **a.** The victims of vampire bats are often asleep at the time of the attack, since the bats are most active at night.

   ☐ **b.** Because it is usually nighttime when vampire bats attack, victims frequently fall asleep after the attack.

   ☐ **c.** Vampire bats must be asleep in order to attack their victims, so the attacks usually occur at night.

D Make Inferences

The following inferences about the article may or may not be correct. Label the statements using the following key:

| **C** Correct Inference | **F** Faulty Inference |

_____ **1.** People who travel to Mexico or Central America will almost always see vampire bats.

_____ **2.** In 1999 some of the people in Nicaragua slept with their windows open and there were no screens on the windows.

_____ **3.** If a vampire bat bites you when you are in a city, you don't have to worry about getting rabies.

_____ **4.** Vampire bats sometimes bite humans when they are frightened, especially after they have been captured.

_____ **5.** Vampire bats rarely have direct contact with other vampire bats.

E Recognize Author's Effect and Intentions

Put an X in the box next to the answer.

1. What is the author's purpose in writing "Night Killers"?
   - ☐ **a.** to inform the reader about vampire bats
   - ☐ **b.** to encourage the reader to protect vampire bats from hunters so that the bats do not become extinct
   - ☐ **c.** to persuade readers to travel to Nicaragua and kill as many vampire bats as possible

2. What does the author imply by saying "Bats were forced out of their rural homes and into places where people lived"?
   - ☐ **a.** People in rural areas are often attacked by bats.
   - ☐ **b.** Very few people live in rural areas.
   - ☐ **c.** Bats usually stay away from humans.

F Evaluate and Create

Put an X in the box next to the answer.

1. From the article, you can predict that every time there is serious flooding in Nicaragua,
   - ☐ **a.** none of the people of Nicaragua will be able to sleep at night until all the vampire bats are killed.
   - ☐ **b.** vampire bats will be a threat.
   - ☐ **c.** farmers will kill their animals for food before vampire bats can attack the animals.

2. If you were a parent in Central America, how could you best use the information in the article to keep your family safe?
   - ☐ **a.** keep my windows closed at night after heavy rains
   - ☐ **b.** make sure my family ate a lot of garlic
   - ☐ **c.** stay awake every night watching for bats

3. What did you have to do to answer question 2?
   - ☐ **a.** find a comparison (how things are the same)
   - ☐ **b.** find a description (how something looks)
   - ☐ **c.** draw a conclusion (a sensible statement based on the text and your experience)

Unit 2 · Lesson 2.5

Escape to Freedom

Frederick Douglass was born a slave in Maryland in 1817. After his daring escape on a train from Maryland to Pennsylvania in 1838, he became a free man. This portrait of Douglass was made in 1848.

**Before You Read
Build Background**

When you don't know much about a topic, you can look for information about it before you read. To build background for this article, you can work with classmates to find information about:

- Frederick Douglass.
- slavery in the United States.

Escape to Freedom

fending for
caring for

1   Frederick Douglass's mother died when he was just six years old. Douglass, who was a slave, ended up **fending for** himself. Every day he did the chores his masters required. At night he slept on the dirt floor of an old shack. He had no shoes, no coat, not even a decent pair of pants. He rarely got enough to eat. To fill his stomach, he sometimes took an egg from the barn or an ear of corn from the field. Other times he fought the dogs for crumbs from under the masters' table.

2   In 1826, when he was eight years old, his Maryland owners sent him to the city of Baltimore. There he went to work for Hugh and Sophia Auld. The Aulds treated him kindly. They gave him food, clothes, and a warm bed to sleep in. Sophia Auld even began teaching him to read, but her husband soon put a stop to that. Once enslaved people learned to read, he warned, they would start getting ideas out of books. Then they would become unhappy with their lives as enslaved people. They might even figure out a way to get free.

3   Douglass heard what Hugh Auld said. He decided to keep working on his reading, no matter what. As the years passed, Douglass found ways to improve his reading skills. He read old papers. He read posters and signs. At the age of 12, he paid 50 cents to buy his first book. One of the stories in the book was about an enslaved person who read so well and knew so much that he was able to talk his master into setting him free. That story gave Douglass even more **incentive** to become a good reader.

incentive
reason

4   By 1838 Hugh Auld had died, and Frederick Douglass had been sent to work in a Baltimore shipyard. It was there that he put together a **bold** plan. He decided to make a run for freedom. In order to succeed, he would have to get out of Maryland.

bold
brave

He would have to make it to one of the northern states, where slavery was illegal. Douglass knew that if he were caught he would be whipped and chained. He might even be killed. He was willing to risk death for the chance to be free.

5   Douglass already knew some African Americans who were free. Known as "freemen," each of them carried "free papers." The documents proved that the holder was free and not a slave. Once in a while, an enslaved person would borrow someone's "free papers" to make an escape. When the runaway reached a free state, he or she would send the papers back. The trick was to get the papers from someone who looked like you. The papers stated such things as height, weight, color of skin, any scars, and so forth.

6   Douglass did not know any freemen who looked like him. He did have an African American friend who was a sailor. This man had a set of papers stating that he was a free American sailor. At the top of the page was an American eagle. It looked very impressive. Douglass thought that these papers might work like "free papers." Unfortunately, the papers called for someone with skin much darker than Douglass's. Douglass decided it was worth a chance. He would use the sailor's papers to make a break for freedom.

7   From Maryland the nearest free state was Pennsylvania. The best way to get there was by train. But Douglass couldn't just walk into the train station and buy a ticket. His papers would be checked too closely. So he waited until the train was pulling out of the station. Only then did he hop on board. He was dressed in a borrowed sailor's suit. He tried to look calm, but every nerve inside his body was on edge.

8   After a while, the conductor began checking tickets. When he got to the car carrying African Americans,

he also checked their papers. The conductor acted rude to some of the people in the car. This made Douglass even more nervous. The conductor's face **brightened** when he got to Douglass. Perhaps it was because of the sailor's uniform. Most Americans had kind feelings for sailors at this time.

brightened
cheered up

9   Still, the conductor had a job to do, so he said to Douglass, "I suppose you have your free papers?"

10   "No, sir," answered Douglass. "I never carry my free papers to sea with me."

11   "But you have something to show that you are a freeman, haven't you?"

12   "Yes, sir," said Douglass, "I have a paper with the American eagle on it."

13   Douglass handed over his papers to the conductor. The man barely glanced at them. He took Douglass's ticket money and left. Douglass was thrilled, but he was not out of danger yet. He was still in Maryland. He might be discovered and arrested at any moment. "I saw on the train several persons who would have known me in any other clothes," wrote Douglass. Amazingly, the sailor's uniform seemed to fool them all.

14   Slowly, the train moved north. To Frederick Douglass the minutes seemed like hours. At one station Douglass looked out the window and caught his breath. Just a few feet away was a man named Captain McGowan. Douglass had done work for him earlier that week. If McGowan noticed him, Douglass's plan would be **foiled**. Luckily, McGowan didn't look Douglass's way.

foiled
ruined

15   "This was not my only hair-breadth escape," wrote Douglass. At one point a German blacksmith who knew Douglass well looked straight at him. After a few seconds, he went back about his business. "I really believe he knew me," wrote Douglass, "but had no heart to betray me."

16 At last Douglass reached Philadelphia, Pennsylvania. Quietly but joyfully, he moved on to New York City. In less than 24 hours, he had gone from being an enslaved person to being a free man. "No man now had a right to call me his slave," wrote Douglass.

17 Douglass kept the details of his escape a secret for more than 40 years. He didn't want to hurt other slaves who might use the same plan. Escaping was hard enough without giving away any secrets to slave owners. Also, Douglass didn't want to cause trouble for anyone who had helped him. Helping an enslaved person to escape was a high crime. As Douglass said, "Murder itself was not more sternly punished."

18 Frederick Douglass went on to become world famous. He spent years fighting slavery. He published his own newspaper, called *The North Star*. Douglass wrote best-selling books about his life. He made friends with white leaders such as Abraham Lincoln. He urged the president to free the slaves. In 1863 Lincoln freed all the slaves in the southern states. So Douglass, who died in 1895, lived to see his people freed.

19 Over the years Frederick Douglass was often asked how his first day of freedom felt. He said, "I felt as one might feel upon escape from a den of hungry lions." He added, "My chains were broken, and the victory brought me unspeakable joy."

If you have been timed while reading this article, enter your reading time below. Then turn to the Words-per-Minute table on page 121 and look up your reading speed (words per minute). Enter your reading speed on the graph on page 122.

Timed Reading

Reading Time: Lesson 2.5　　　_____ : _____

　　　　　　　　　　　　　　　Minutes　Seconds

COMPREHENSION & CRITICAL THINKING SKILLS

A Recognize and Recall Details

Put an X in the box next to the answer that correctly completes each statement.

1. When Douglass was sent to work for the Aulds in Maryland,
   - ☐ a. he slept on the dirt floor of an old shack.
   - ☐ b. Sophia Auld began teaching him to read.
   - ☐ c. he worked in a shipyard.
2. While Douglass was working in a Baltimore shipyard, he
   - ☐ a. made a plan to escape to the North.
   - ☐ b. decided to run to Pennsylvania.
   - ☐ c. thought he might be killed.
3. Many slaves who wanted to be free
   - ☐ a. became sailors.
   - ☐ b. borrowed a free person's "free papers."
   - ☐ c. took trains to the North.
4. When Douglass was on the train to Pennsylvania,
   - ☐ a. he was wearing a borrowed sailor's suit.
   - ☐ b. the train conductor was rude to him.
   - ☐ c. some people recognized him.

B Find the Main Idea

One statement below expresses the main idea of the article. One statement is too general, and another is too narrow. Label the statements using the following key:

M Main Idea	B Too Broad	N Too Narrow

____ 1. Frederick Douglass was an enslaved person who escaped to the North to freedom.

____ 2. Frederick Douglass learned to read from Sophia Auld, his owner.

____ 3. Frederick Douglass escaped from slavery on a dangerous journey north by train using borrowed papers from a friend who was a free American sailor.

C Summarize and Paraphrase

1. Choose the summary that says the most important things about the article in the fewest words.

   ☐ **a.** Frederick Douglass was born a slave. One of his masters started to teach him to read. Some of the things he read gave him the idea that he could be free. One day he made a run for freedom. He escaped to the North and became world famous.

   ☐ **b.** Even though Frederick Douglass was born a slave, he learned to read, made a daring run for freedom, and became a world-famous writer and an advocate for ending slavery.

   ☐ **c.** Frederick Douglass escaped to the North and became a famous writer. He lived to see Abraham Lincoln free the slaves in 1863.

2. Read the statement and the paraphrase of that statement. Choose the reason that best tells why the paraphrase does not say the same thing as the statement.

   Statement: "That story gave Douglass even more incentive to become a good reader."

   Paraphrase: That story helped Douglass to become a good reader.

   ☐ **a.** The paraphrase says too much.

   ☐ **b.** The paraphrase doesn't say enough.

   ☐ **c.** The paraphrase doesn't agree with the statement from the article.

D Make Inferences

The following inferences about the article may or may not be correct. Label the statements using the following key:

C Correct Inference	**F** Faulty Inference

_____ **1.** Frederick Douglass did not know who his father was.

_____ **2.** Many free African Americans helped enslaved African Americans gain their freedom.

_____ **3.** Enslaved people often worked for several different owners during their lives.

_____ **4.** It was legal for enslaved people to ride trains without papers.

_____ **5.** In Douglass's time, African Americans had to ride in separate cars on trains.

E Recognize Author's Effect and Intentions

Put an X in the box next to the answer.

1. The main purpose of the first paragraph is to
   - ☐ **a.** describe the life of an enslaved person.
   - ☐ **b.** describe Frederick Douglass's background.
   - ☐ **c.** express an opinion about slavery.

2. What does the author imply by saying, "Other times he fought the dogs for crumbs from under the masters' table"?
   - ☐ **a.** Douglass was always fed the same food as the dogs.
   - ☐ **b.** Douglass's master thought he was less valuable than a dog.
   - ☐ **c.** Douglass was so hungry that he would eat the food that fell from his masters' table.

3. The author probably wrote this article in order to
   - ☐ **a.** make people aware of the terrible conditions in which many enslaved people lived.
   - ☐ **b.** inform people about Frederick Douglass and his brave escape.
   - ☐ **c.** explain why the owners of slaves didn't want them to learn to read.

F Evaluate and Create

Put an X in the box next to the answer.

1. From what Douglass said, you can conclude that
   - ☐ **a.** not many enslaved people knew how to read.
   - ☐ **b.** most enslaved people lived in the North.
   - ☐ **c.** most enslaved people going north went to Pennsylvania.

2. What did you have to do to answer question 1?
   - ☐ **a.** find a cause (why something happened)
   - ☐ **b.** find a reason (why something is the way it is)
   - ☐ **c.** draw a conclusion (a statement based on the text)

3. Into which of the following theme categories would this story best fit?
   - ☐ **a.** enslaved people in America
   - ☐ **b.** trains in the 1800s
   - ☐ **c.** from slavery to freedom

Unit 3 · Lesson 3.1
A Horrible Way to Die

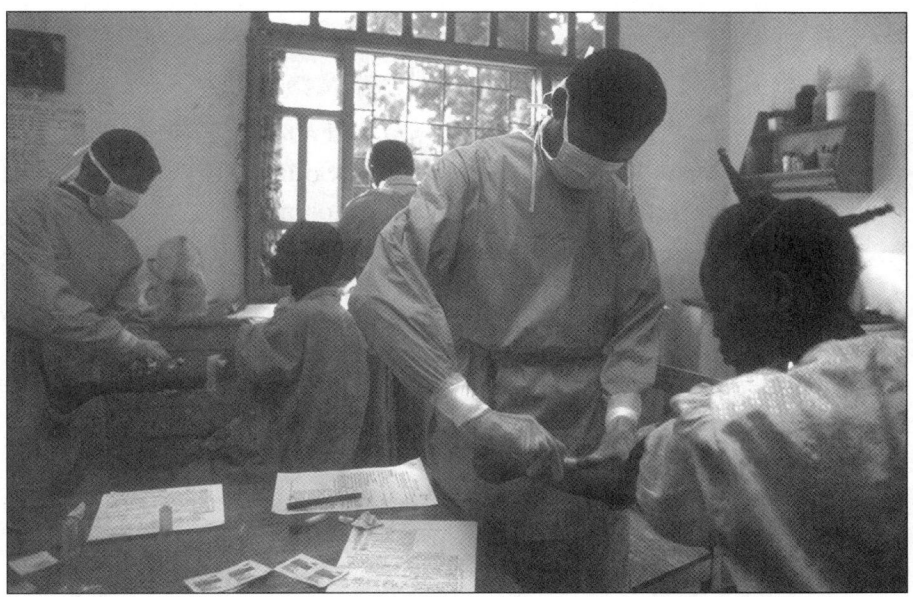

In 1995 the deadly Ebola virus broke out in Kikwit, Zaire. Hundreds of people died horrendous deaths. Doctors knew that the disease spread through contact with a victim's blood. Here doctors are taking blood samples from some of the victims.

Before You Read
Preview

Previewing the lesson gives you an idea of what you are going to read. To preview the lesson:

- read the title and the photo caption.
- skim the article to get a general idea of what it is about.
- read the questions after the article.

A Horrible Way to Die

1   36-year-old Kimfumu had a fever. His head ached. And he had diarrhea. So in early April 1995 Kimfumu went to the main hospital in Kikwit, Zaire (present-day Democratic Republic of the Congo). Doctors thought he had an infection in his intestines. They treated him for it, but over the next two days he grew worse. At last, doctors chose to operate. They hoped to fix whatever was wrong inside Kimfumu's belly.

2   The operation turned into a nightmare. When doctors opened Kimfumu up, they found his insides were dissolving. His organs were literally turning to mush. There was nothing doctors could do to help him. They sewed him back up and tried to ease his pain. A nun named Sister Floralba took over his care. She knew about his condition. In fact, she had been present during the operation. As Sister Floralba watched in horror, blood began to pour from Kimfumu's nose. His ears and even his eyes began to bleed. On April 14, Kimfumu died.

3   By then, Sister Floralba herself was feeling ill. She, too, developed a fever. She, too, had a headache and diarrhea. Three of her friends, all of them nuns, did what they could. They drove Sister Floralba 50 miles to a bigger hospital. Within days, she died the same **horrifying** death as Kimfumu.

horrifying
frightening

4   The next day, Sister Floralba's three friends became sick. One by one, they all died. By then, doctors realized what was happening. Some terrible disease was spreading through Kikwit. Each day, new cases came in. Victims all showed the same **hideous** symptoms. A few survived, but most were dying.

hideous
ugly

5   Doctors took blood samples from some of the victims. They rushed the samples to the United States. Doctors at the Centers for Disease Control (CDC) in Atlanta, Georgia, studied the samples. On May 11, CDC doctors announced their findings. They had figured out what was causing the deaths in Kikwit. It was the dreaded Ebola virus.

6   Ebola was first identified in 1976. At that time, it had killed about 400 people in another part of Zaire. Doctors knew the virus was deadly. They knew it spread through contact with a victim's blood. However, they didn't know how the virus got into human blood in the first place. Dr. Peter Piot was one of the doctors who discovered Ebola. As he said in 1995, "Where Ebola comes from is a very big question mark."

7   Many doctors, including Dr. Piot, think Ebola comes from deep within Africa's rain forests. It may live in the body of some rodent or insect there. The virus probably does not harm this "host" creature. As long as the host has no contact with human beings, everything is fine; but now people are cutting down rain forests. So hosts and humans are meeting. As they do, the virus has a chance to enter the human body. While the virus does not hurt the host, it is deadly to humans.

8   After the 1976 outbreak, the virus faded back into the rain forest, but then, in 1995, it returned. By the

time Sister Floralba's three friends died, terror filled the streets of Kikwit. Few people knew exactly what was happening, but they saw that death was happening all around them. By mid-May, 77 people had died. Each day, that number climbed higher.

9   Doctors from around the world rushed to Kikwit to help. A **horrendous** mess awaited them. The hospital where Kimfumu died was filthy. "People were vomiting," said one U.S. doctor. "There was . . . blood all over the floors and walls. The dead were lying among the living." There were no masks, no gowns, no clean instruments. Given the conditions, it was easy to see how virus-filled blood had passed from one person to the next.

10   There was another problem as well. By the time outside doctors arrived, many patients and staff members had fled in fear. That raised a chilling question. Were these runaways spreading the disease to other places? Would Ebola soon break out in bigger cities? Would it become a worldwide plague?

11   For days, people everywhere held their breath. It could take the virus up to 21 days to produce symptoms in a victim, so no one knew just how far it had spread. The government of Zaire closed all the schools in Kikwit. Medical clinics were also closed. Officials ordered people to stay in their homes. Still, every day, more and more cases were reported.

12   Meanwhile, medical teams **fanned out** to nearby villages. They tried to explain the danger to people there. They begged the villagers to treat their sick carefully. They pleaded with families to **refrain from** normal burial customs. Those customs involved handling the bloody organs of the dead person. If family members insisted on a normal burial, doctors urged them to wear rubber gloves.

horrendous
terrible; nasty

fanned out
spread out

refrain from
skip

13 Some people tried to do what the medical teams said. Other simply threw up their hands. "It's useless for us to do anything," said one villager. "What can we do against this disease?" Still others heard the news too late. A man named Mola had just finished burying his father when a medical team found him. "I don't know what to say," said Mola. "I am the one who helped my father. I have already touched the body. Now you tell me I must avoid contact?"

14 By May 26, 121 people had died of Ebola. Three weeks later, the number was up to 220. By July, it had gone to 315, but then—luckily—the virus died out. All the people who had been exposed to Ebola had either died or fought it off. By August 24, the epidemic was over.

15 Officials believe the Ebola virus still lurks in Africa's rain forests. It is still there, hiding, in some host creature. We don't know what that host is. We don't know when, if ever, Ebola will infect more human bodies. Still, the threat of Ebola is a real one. It is one more reason why we should think twice before cutting down the world's remaining rain forests.

....

If you have been timed while reading this article, enter your reading time below. Then turn to the Words-per-Minute table on page 121 and look up your reading speed (words per minute). Enter your reading speed on the graph on page 122.

Timed Reading

Reading Time: Lesson 3.1

_____ : _____
Minutes   Seconds

COMPREHENSION & CRITICAL THINKING SKILLS

A Recognize and Recall Details

Put an X in the box next to the answer that correctly completes each statement about the article.

1. Some of the symptoms of Kimfumu's illness were
   - ☐ a. fever and diarrhea.
   - ☐ b. dizziness and loss of memory.
   - ☐ c. loss of the use of his legs and arms.

2. Doctors rushed blood samples to the Centers for Disease Control in
   - ☐ a. Cairo, Egypt.
   - ☐ b. New York City.
   - ☐ c. Atlanta, Georgia.

3. Some doctors believe the Ebola virus comes from
   - ☐ a. improperly cooked meat.
   - ☐ b. an insect or rodent in the rain forest.
   - ☐ c. worms in garbage.

4. The Ebola virus is spread through
   - ☐ a. contact with a victim's blood.
   - ☐ b. coughs, sneezes, and handshakes.
   - ☐ c. worm bites.

5. In 1976 in another part of Zaire, the Ebola virus had killed about
   - ☐ a. 40,000 people.
   - ☐ b. 4,000 people.
   - ☐ c. 400 people.

B Find the Main Idea

One of the statements below expresses the main idea of the article. One statement is too broad. The other statement is too narrow. Label the statements using the following key:

M Main Idea	**B** Too Broad	**N** Too Narrow

_____ 1. The Ebola virus caused one of the most dangerous and mysterious diseases to appear in years.

_____ 2. Doctors who operated on the first of the Ebola virus's victims, Kimfumu, discovered that his organs were dissolving.

_____ 3. The Ebola virus that struck Kikwit in 1995 killed hundreds and left Africans in fear that it could strike again.

86 Reading Basics · Intermediate 1 Reader

C Summarize and Paraphrase

1. Reread paragraph 9 in the article. Write a summary of the paragraph in no more than 25 words.

   _____
   _____
   _____
   _____

   Now shorten your summary of paragraph 9 to 15 words or less.

   _____
   _____
   _____

2. Choose the sentence that correctly restates the following sentence from the article: "By the time outside doctors arrived, many patients and staff members had fled in fear."

   ☐ **a.** When doctors from other countries arrived, many patients and staff ran away from them.

   ☐ **b.** When outside doctors got there, they discovered that many patients and staff members had run away because they were so afraid.

   ☐ **c.** Fearing the worst, outside doctors escaped along with many patients and staff members.

D Make Inferences

The following inferences about the article may or may not be correct. Label the statements using the following key:

C Correct Inference	**F** Faulty Inference

_____ 1. The Ebola virus kills its victims quickly.

_____ 2. Doctors believe that viruses are not able to travel through rubber gloves.

_____ 3. Cutting down large sections of the rain forest would stop the Ebola virus from spreading.

_____ 4. The Ebola virus is a danger only in Kikwit.

_____ 5. The Ebola virus is found not only in African rain forests but in South American and Asian rain forests as well.

E Recognize Author's Effect and Intentions

Put an **X** in the box next to the answer.

1. What is the author's purpose in writing "A Horrible Way to Die"?
   - ☐ **a.** to encourage readers to become doctors
   - ☐ **b.** to inform readers about a frightening disease that struck the people of Zaire
   - ☐ **c.** to express an opinion about medical care in Zaire

2. From the statements below, choose the one that you believe the author would agree with.
   - ☐ **a.** Officials in Zaire never took the Ebola danger seriously.
   - ☐ **b.** People should keep cutting down rain forests.
   - ☐ **c.** Doctors in Zaire were glad to have the help of doctors who came from other countries.

3. Judging by statements from the article "A Horrible Way to Die," you can conclude that the author wants the reader to think that
   - ☐ **a.** the Ebola virus is not dangerous.
   - ☐ **b.** only Africans need to worry about dying of the Ebola virus.
   - ☐ **c.** the Ebola virus could become a threat to human beings once again.

F Evaluate and Create

Put an **X** in the box next to the answer.

1. Which of the following statements is an opinion?
   - ☐ **a.** It's useless for us to do anything about the Ebola virus.
   - ☐ **b.** Ebola was first identified in 1976.
   - ☐ **c.** By May 26, 121 people had died of Ebola.

2. If you were a doctor, you could use the information in the article to
   - ☐ **a.** plan further research on the Ebola virus.
   - ☐ **b.** create a virus that would be less dangerous than Ebola.
   - ☐ **c.** end the danger of Ebola forever.

3. After reading the article, you can predict that
   - ☐ **a.** the Ebola virus will soon die out forever.
   - ☐ **b.** the Ebola virus will return someday and kill more people.
   - ☐ **c.** in the future, the Ebola virus will not be dangerous to humans.

Unit 3 · Lesson 3.2

A Shocking Experience

Lightning bolts coming from low storm clouds hit the ground. Although people rarely get struck by lightning, it does happen.

Before You Read
Use Prior Knowledge

Connecting what you already know with what you read makes remembering new material easier. Ask yourself:

- Why is it important to stay inside during a thunderstorm?
- What makes lightning dangerous?

A Shocking Experience

1   It could happen to you almost anywhere. You could be walking along the golf course. You could be enjoying an outdoor picnic or sailing on the open water. It could also happen as you talk on the phone, wash the dishes, or even watch TV. However, the odds are very much against it. Only one person in about 600,000 ever gets struck by lightning.

2   Given those numbers, you'd have to call any lightning victim unlucky, but what do you call a person who has been hit *seven* times? Incredibly unlucky? Then that's what you'd have to call Roy Sullivan. Between 1942 and 1977, he was struck by lightning seven times. It's a world record.

3   Sullivan worked as a park ranger in Virginia. His first encounter with lightning cost him a big toe. Later hits scorched his eyebrows, singed his hair, and burned his shoulder. In 1973 Sullivan suffered the worst hit of his life. He was stepping out of his truck when lightning streaked toward him. "It set my hat and hair on fire," he later said. "Then it went down my left arm and leg, knocked off my shoe, and crossed over to my right leg. It also set my underwear on fire."

4   Despite Sullivan's record, Virginia is not the state with the most lightning. That distinction belongs to Florida. The peninsula of Florida lies between two warm bodies of water. High humidity and hot weather **breed** many violent storms. It is really bad

breed
create

during the hottest time of the year. That's when the "Sunshine State" **gets bombarded with** thunderstorms and lightning. About 5 million bolts of lightning strike Florida each year. That is far more than in any other state.

gets bombarded with
gets hit heavily by

5   Lightning kills people every year. It also does some strange things to people who get hit and somehow live. Take the case of Florida's George McBay. One day in 1993 he was helping to lower a large metal pipe from a roof. Suddenly, he was struck by lightning. "It felt like everything in my body just blew out the top of my head," he said.

6   The lightning bolt didn't kill McBay, but it changed his life forever. "The best day that I've had since the accident isn't as good as the worst day I had before the accident," McBay later said. "You get lost. Blackouts. A good day is lying on the couch."

7   Sherri Spain could sympathize with McBay. On August 27, 1989, Spain was in Maryville, Tennessee. She and her volleyball team were taking a lunch break outside a gym. As they ate, a storm rolled in. Spain really liked storms. She liked the crack of thunder and the flash of lightning. "My heart races during a storm," she once said.

8   When the wind began to blow and the rain came, Spain stood just outside the gym with Dawn Platt, one of her students. All the other students ran for cover back inside the gym. "It was stupid," she later admitted.

9   A lightning bolt hit the steel door directly behind Spain and entered the back of her head. She slumped to the ground. Platt knelt beside her, not knowing what to do. "I held her hand and called her name, but she didn't respond," Platt later recalled. "I thought

she was dead. All I could do was scream for help and pray."

10   Spain lived, but the lightning affected her in many ways. She lost sight in her right eye and hearing in her right ear. Her hair, which had been dark brown, turned blond. She developed heart trouble. Spain also lost much of her brain power. As a teacher, Spain had always valued her mental abilities. Yet suddenly she couldn't even remember the letters of the alphabet. It took her a year of **grueling** work to rebuild her basic skills. Even then she still had memory problems. She couldn't remember facts or dates. When she finally returned to the classroom, Spain spent hours each night preparing her lessons and had to use lots of notes.

grueling
difficult

11   It may seem hard to believe, but once in a great while being struck by lightning can be a blessing. In February 1971 Edwin Robinson lost control of his truck and crashed on an icy road in Maine. His head went through the back window. As a result, he suffered brain damage. Slowly, he lost his sight and much of his hearing. He had to learn Braille and wear a hearing aid. Robinson lived this way for 9 years.

12   Then, on June 4, 1980, Robinson went for a short walk in the rain with his aluminum cane. Without warning, a bolt of lightning hit him and knocked him out. For 20 minutes, he lay unconscious on the ground. At last he woke up and returned to his house. He felt very tired, but otherwise he seemed fine. He decided to take a nap.

remarkable
amazing

13   Then something **remarkable** happened. When he woke up from his nap, he could read the time on the kitchen clock. He hadn't been able to do that for 9 years. Within a few days, he could see well enough to walk without a cane. His hearing also improved

greatly. He even began to regrow some hair on his bald head.

14   Edwin Robinson's case is a rare exception. You don't want to test your luck by running around in a thunderstorm waving a golf club over your head. You should always treat lightning for what it is— a potential killer. Hurricanes and tornadoes make the news because they tend to kill in large numbers. Lightning **picks off** its victims one at a time. In the end, though, lightning kills more Americans than almost any other weather hazard.

picks off
kills

15   The odds of getting struck by a bolt of lightning are still about as high as winning the lottery. However, unlike the lottery, looking for lightning bolts is a game most people would rather not play.

....

If you have been timed while reading this article, enter your reading time below. Then turn to the Words-per-Minute table on page 121 and look up your reading speed (words per minute). Enter your reading speed on the graph on page 122.

Timed Reading

Reading Time: Lesson 3.2

_____ : _____
Minutes   Seconds

COMPREHENSION & CRITICAL THINKING SKILLS

A Recognize and Recall Details

Put an **X** in the box next to the answer that correctly completes each statement about the article.

1. When Roy Sullivan was struck by lightning in 1973,
   - ☐ **a.** it scorched his eyebrows.
   - ☐ **b.** it set his hat and hair on fire.
   - ☐ **c.** he lost a big toe.
2. The state with the most lightning is
   - ☐ **a.** Florida.
   - ☐ **b.** Virginia.
   - ☐ **c.** Tennessee.
3. After being hit by lightning, Sherri Spain
   - ☐ **a.** lost sight in her left eye.
   - ☐ **b.** could not return to teaching.
   - ☐ **c.** had memory problems.
4. After Edwin Robinson was hit by lightning, he
   - ☐ **a.** went for another short walk in the rain to see if anyone else had been hit by lightning.
   - ☐ **b.** needed a cane to walk.
   - ☐ **c.** regained his sight and hearing.

B Find the Main Idea

One of the statements below expresses the main idea of the article. One statement is too broad. The other statement is too narrow—it explains only part of the article. Label the statements using the following key:

| **M** Main Idea | **B** Too Broad | **N** Too Narrow |

_____ 1. People have been struck by lightning, but it doesn't happen very often.

_____ 2. Roy Sullivan was struck by lightning seven times in 35 years.

_____ 3. Getting struck by lightning, while it is not likely, can affect people in both good and bad ways.

C Summarize and Paraphrase

1. Look for the important ideas and events in paragraphs 5 and 6. Summarize those paragraphs in about 25 words.

   _____
   _____
   _____
   _____
   _____

2. Complete the following one-sentence summary of the article: "The article begins with figures about the odds of being struck by lightning, continues with stories about times when people were struck by lightning, and ends with
   - [ ] a. a warning about how dangerous lightning can be."
   - [ ] b. the story of yet another person who was hit by lightning."
   - [ ] c. more figures about the odds of being hit by lightning."

3. Choose the sentence that correctly restates the following sentence from the article: "High humidity and hot weather breed many violent storms."
   - [ ] a. The combination of high humidity and hot weather create many terrible storms.
   - [ ] b. In hot and humid weather there are fewer bad storms.
   - [ ] c. Violent storms cause the weather to become hot and humid, which causes lightning.

D Make Inferences

The following inferences about the article may or may not be correct. Label the statements using the following key:

C Correct Inference	**F** Faulty Inference

_____ 1. During a lightning storm, it's safer to be indoors.

_____ 2. When people are struck by lightning, they are almost always in a forest or a park.

_____ 3. Some people attract lightning more than others.

_____ 4. Lightning is drawn to metal objects.

_____ 5. When lightning hits people, it always affects the brain.

E Recognize Author's Effect and Intentions
Put an **X** in the box next to the answer.
1. The author uses the first sentence of the article to
   - ☐ **a.** entertain the reader.
   - ☐ **b.** get the reader's attention.
   - ☐ **c.** describe the qualities of lightning.
2. What is the author's purpose in writing "A Shocking Experience"?
   - ☐ **a.** to warn of the danger of lightning strikes
   - ☐ **b.** to express an opinion about lightning strikes
   - ☐ **c.** to describe the effects of being hit by lightning
3. What does the author imply with the statement, "You don't want to test your luck by running around in a thunderstorm waving a golf club over your head"?
   - ☐ **a.** It is impossible to play golf during a thunderstorm.
   - ☐ **b.** Golf clubs attract lightning.
   - ☐ **c.** Motion attracts lightning.

F Evaluate and Create
1. Which of the following statements is an opinion?
   - ☐ **a.** One person in about 600,000 gets struck by lightning.
   - ☐ **b.** Roy Sullivan worked as a park ranger.
   - ☐ **c.** Anyone who gets struck by lightning more than seven times is one of the most unlucky people in the world.
2. List ways in which Edwin Robinson's and Sherri Spain's experiences after being struck by lightning were similar and different.

   Similarities

   _____
   _____

   Differences

   _____
   _____

Unit 3 · Lesson 3.3

Needles That Cure

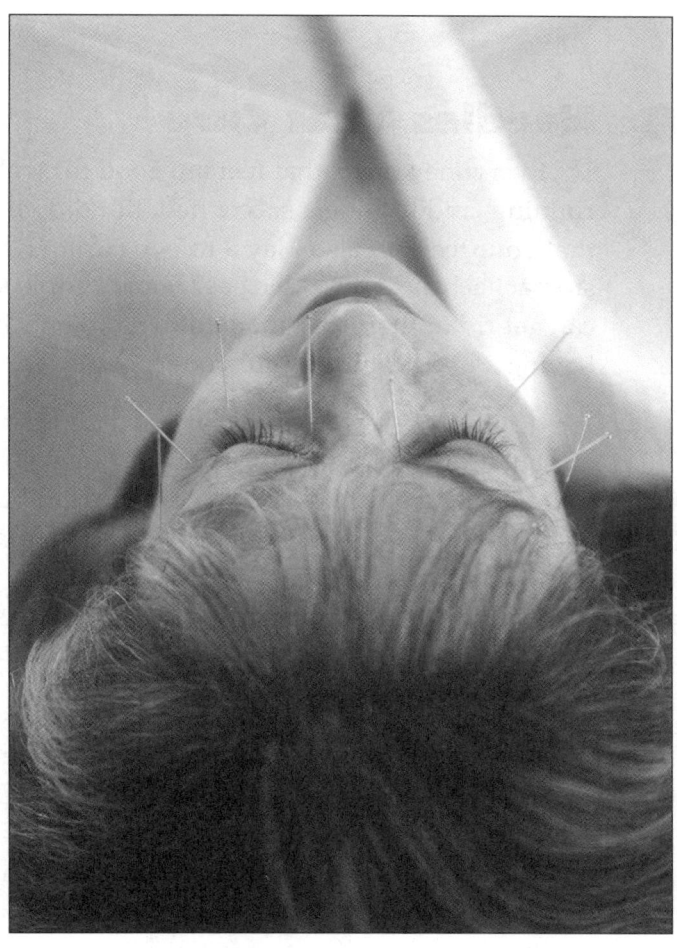

Acupuncture is the ancient Chinese practice of inserting special needles into the body to cure various ills. Acupuncture is now familiar to the western world, where practitioners use it to treat many different problems, such as nausea, asthma, and neck pains.

Before You Read
Ask Questions

Thinking of specific questions before you read can make an article more interesting. Follow these steps:
- Read the photo caption and the title and look at the photo.
- In a notebook, write questions you have about acupuncture.
- As you read the article, find answers to your questions.

Needles That Cure

1 Everyone knows that feet are good for walking, running, and kicking a soccer ball. But did you know that your feet can also play a role in curing headaches, stomachaches, and toothaches? Some people say you can get rid of these and many other ailments just by having a needle jabbed into your foot.

2 It sounds crazy at first. However, according to the ancient art of acupuncture, it works. A needle stuck into a specific point on your second toe can **banish** headaches. A needle between your second and third toes can rid you of a sore throat. A needle put into the outside of your foot can **stimulate** your vision.

banish
drive away

stimulate
excite to activity

3 Acupuncture began in China more than 4,000 years ago. It is based on the belief that there is a natural flow of energy inside each human being. This energy, or life force, is called *qi* (pronounced CHEE). The qi is said to flow along certain pathways in the body. These pathways, called meridians, are like rivers. When they flow freely, you feel strong and healthy. However, if one of your meridians gets blocked, the flow of energy is **disrupted**. Your qi becomes unbalanced. Too much qi builds up in one part of your body. Other parts don't get enough. That's where the needles come in. When inserted in just the right spots, they can unblock your meridians and get your qi flowing correctly again.

disrupted
disturbed or upset

4   No one has ever been able to prove the existence of these energy pathways. Over the years Chinese practitioners have fine-tuned their view of qi. They have identified 14 meridians. They have named about 1,500 points on the body where these meridians can get **clogged**. They have figured out which points need to be opened to relieve different pains. Let's say your immune system is weak. In that case you'll need a needle put in near your elbow. If nausea is your problem, the needle must go lower down on your arm, right near your wrist.

clogged
blocked

5   When people in Europe and America first heard about acupuncture, they were skeptical. For a long time they paid no attention to stories about it, but by the 1970s some doctors were taking a closer look. Some of them began to experiment with it. What they found surprised them. Many patients said that acupuncture lessened their pain. When nothing else would work, it often gave them relief.

6   One woman was suffering from asthma. Her doctor gave her medicine, but it made her body swell up like a balloon. Soon she weighed 300 pounds. The asthma attacks kept coming. As soon as she started acupuncture treatment, though, the asthma went away. The woman lost 80 pounds and was able to throw away all her asthma medicine.

7   Another patient had neck pain that she could not shake. After a year of **misery**, she turned to acupuncture. "All of a sudden, the pain was gone," she said.

misery
suffering

8   Does this mean that the Chinese view of energy pathways is accurate? Maybe not. Western doctors have another theory about why acupuncture works. They have found that sticking needles into the body can stimulate the nervous system. The nervous

system then releases chemicals into your body. Many doctors think it is these chemicals that take away the pain.

9   Some people have said that acupuncture is all in your head. That is, it only works because you expect it to work. However, that idea would not explain why acupuncture works on animals. Cows, dogs, cats, and horses have all been helped by acupuncture. Certainly these animals were not true believers!

10   Acupuncture has also worked on many humans who didn't think it would. One such patient was Zang-Hee Cho. Cho was a California physicist. In 1993 he fell while hiking on a mountain. He hurt his back so badly he could barely walk. Some of his relatives said he should try acupuncture, but he scoffed at the idea. He didn't think there was anything to it. When he finally agreed to give it a try, he was amazed. "After about 10 minutes, I felt the pain melting away," he said.

11   Cho later set up a study to find out how acupuncture affects the brain. He watched needles being put into patients' feet. The goal was to unclog the qi that flowed to the eyes. That sounded like nonsense to Cho. He took pictures of the patients' brains during the procedure. He was shocked. Their brains showed the same activity as when a light was shone in their eyes. "I never thought anything would happen," Cho said, "but it's very clear that stimulating the acupuncture point triggers activity in the visual cortex part of the brain."

12   Other studies have found that acupuncture increases the flow of blood to the brain. It sends more blood to the part of the brain that registers pain. Thanks to studies like these, more and more people are lining up for treatment. The World Health

Organization has even drawn up a list of ailments that can be treated this way. The list has everything from chest infections to earaches to back pain.

13 If you should ever try acupuncture, here's what you will find. Up to 20 or more needles will be stuck into various parts of your body. These needles are very thin, and most patients say they don't cause pain. Some of the needles may not be pushed in very far. Others may be put as deep as three inches. The needles will stay in place for 15 to 30 minutes. Practitioners say you might feel relief right away or you might need several sessions to feel better.

14 One word of warning: In most states, acupuncturists don't need medical degrees. So if you think your qi is out of line, be careful. Pick someone who knows what he or she is doing. A bad acupuncturist could damage your nerves or puncture one of your lungs. If that were to happen, you'd be in worse shape than you were when you started.

If you have been timed while reading this article, enter your reading time below. Then turn to the Words-per-Minute table on page 121 and look up your reading speed (words per minute). Enter your reading speed on the graph on page 122.

Timed Reading

Reading Time: Lesson 3.3

_____ : _____
Minutes   Seconds

COMPREHENSION & CRITICAL THINKING SKILLS

A Recognize and Recall Details

Put an X in the box next to the answer that correctly completes each statement about the article.

1. Acupuncture probably started in China about
   - ☐ a. 400 years ago.
   - ☐ b. 4,000 years ago.
   - ☐ c. 10,000 years ago.
2. The term *qi* refers to
   - ☐ a. people trained to do acupuncture.
   - ☐ b. the method of sticking needles at particular body points.
   - ☐ c. the energy, or life force, in every person.
3. A California physicist Zang-Hee Cho turned to acupuncture after he
   - ☐ a. fell while hiking on a mountain.
   - ☐ b. was injured in a car crash.
   - ☐ c. developed severe asthma.
4. Once the needles are inserted into a patient's body, they usually stay there
   - ☐ a. overnight.
   - ☐ b. for only a few seconds.
   - ☐ c. for 15 to 30 minutes.

B Find the Main Idea

One of the statements below expresses the main idea of the article. One statement is too broad. The other statement is too narrow—it explains only part of the article. Label the statements using the following key:

M Main Idea	B Too Broad	N Too Narrow

_____ 1. *Qi* is the Chinese term for the flow of energy that is inside every person all the time.

_____ 2. Acupuncture is an ancient Chinese practice for relieving pain and disease by sticking needles into specific points in a person's body.

_____ 3. Although some medical treatments have been around for centuries, scientists have only now begun to study them.

C Summarize and Paraphrase

1. Reread paragraph 5 on the article. Below, write a summary of the paragraph in no more than 25 words.

   _____
   _____
   _____
   _____

   Now rewrite your summary in 15 words or less.

   _____
   _____

2. Choose the sentence that correctly restates the following sentence from the article: "Thanks to studies like these, more and more people are lining up for acupuncture treatment."

   ☐ a. Acupuncture practitioners are thanking scientists who conducted the studies because more people are asking for acupuncture treatments.

   ☐ b. More people are choosing to try acupuncture because of these studies.

   ☐ c. The acupuncture practitioners are gratefully lining up to be part of these studies.

D Make Inferences

The following inferences about the article may or may not be correct. Label the statements using the following key:

C Correct Inference	F Faulty Inference

____ 1. Western doctors have always been anxious to adopt the medical practices of other cultures.

____ 2. People in pain are willing to take chances with almost any treatment that promises relief.

____ 3. Western doctors don't know everything about how the human body works.

____ 4. Acupuncture practitioners in China are new to western medicine, just as western doctors are new to acupuncture.

____ 5. Chinese practitioners don't use any medical treatments besides acupuncture.

E Recognize Author's Effect and Intentions

Put an **X** in the box next to the answer.

1. What does the author mean by the following statement: "These pathways, called meridians, are like rivers"?
   - ☐ **a.** Qi flows in meridians just as water flows in rivers.
   - ☐ **b.** Meridians carry qi and water around the body.
   - ☐ **c.** Meridians can dry up when there is no qi, just as rivers can dry up when there is no rain.

2. Some people say that acupuncture works only because patients want it to work. Choose the statement below that describes how the author addresses the opposing point of view.
   - ☐ **a.** The author notes that acupuncture has helped animals, who don't understand what it is.
   - ☐ **b.** The author notes that it is often the most desperate people who find relief in acupuncture.
   - ☐ **c.** The author notes that many people desperately want acupuncture to work for them.

F Evaluate and Create

Put an **X** in the box next to the answer.

1. Which sentence expresses an opinion?
   - ☐ **a.** Qi is not an important medical concept.
   - ☐ **b.** Acupuncture has helped some people's pain.
   - ☐ **c.** Chinese practitioners of acupuncture have identified about 1,500 acupuncture points.

2. From the article, you can predict that if western scientists continue to study acupuncture, they will
   - ☐ **a.** decide to stop using western medicine and use only acupuncture to relieve pain.
   - ☐ **b.** improve their understanding of what makes acupuncture work.
   - ☐ **c.** decide that acupuncture doesn't really work for anyone.

Unit 3 · Lesson 3.4

Hanging from a Cliff

Conservationist John Muir (right) was a famous naturalist and mountain climber. Here he poses with President Theodore Roosevelt in California.

Before You Read
Build Background Knowledge

When you don't know much about a topic, you can look for information about it before you read. You can:

- find facts online or in the library about John Muir.
- talk with classmates about mountain climbing.

Hanging from a Cliff

1   S. Hall Young thought it would be fun to climb a mountain. He didn't have much experience, but how hard could it be? After all, he was only 29 years old and in fairly good shape. He did have problems with his shoulders—he had dislocated them 10 years earlier, and they were still weak—but he didn't think that would matter. He didn't plan on putting much weight on his upper body. Besides, he would be climbing with John Muir, the famous naturalist. Muir was known as a smart, strong climber.

2   On a bright summer day in 1879, Young and Muir headed up an 8,000-foot peak in southern Alaska. After three hours, they passed the tree line. They began to scramble over rocks and boulders. Muir set a brutally fast pace. "It was only by **exerting** myself to the limit of my strength that I was able to keep near him," said Young. Yet Young did not complain. He knew that Muir was trying to get them to the top in time to see the sunset.

exerting
pushing

3   By late afternoon they were nearing the summit. However, the most difficult part of the climb still lay ahead of them. It was a wall of rock that seemed to shoot straight up. Young did not see how they could possibly get past it.

4   Muir, however, was **undeterred**. "We must climb **cautiously** here," was all he said. Then he began to climb the wall, finding tiny handholds and footholds as he went. Young followed as best he could, but he could feel his shoulders beginning to ache. "My strength began to fail," he later wrote, "my breath to come in gasps, my muscles to twitch."

undeterred
not afraid

cautiously
carefully

5   At last Young came to the top of the wall. He was now only 50 feet from the peak, but he was exhausted.

Looking down, Young came to a five-foot gap in the trail and saw that the earth **sloped** away sharply for about 12 feet, opening into a thousand-foot crevasse.

sloped
slanted

6   Young's exhaustion made him careless, and as he prepared to jump, he stepped too close to the edge. Suddenly a rock gave way, and Young found himself falling down the 12-foot slope toward the crevasse.

7   Screaming, Young twisted his body around to face the slope. His arms struck the wall of the slope hard and instantly both shoulders became dislocated. "With my paralyzed arms flopping helplessly above my head, I slid swiftly down the narrow chasm," he later wrote. He dug his toes and chin into the gravel, trying desperately to halt his slide.

8   At last he came to a stop. His feet hung out over the crevasse and his arms lay useless above his head. Only by digging into the gravel with his chin was he able to hang on. "Every moment I seemed to be slipping inch by inch," he remembered. "I had no hope of escape at all. The gravel was rattling past me and piling up against my head. The jar of a little rock and all would be over."

9   Suddenly, he heard John Muir's voice above him.

10   "My God!" cried Muir. Then, a few seconds later, Muir called, "Hold fast; I'm going to get you out of this."

11   Muir couldn't get to Young from the far side of the gap, and he couldn't jump across it because the edge had crumbled away, making the gap much wider. Muir had to leave Young and circle around the mountain. It took him 10 minutes to get back to the top of the slope where Young had fallen.

12   By then, Young didn't think he could last another second. Cold wind whipped at his light clothing, and

his shoulders throbbed with pain. It took all his energy to keep his muscles from shaking. He was now hanging so far over the crevasse that any movement could send him to his death.

13   Carefully Muir lowered himself down the slope toward Young. At last he got close enough. He was standing on a narrow ledge. With one hand he held onto a small piece of rock that jutted out from the slope. With the other he grabbed the back of Young's shirt and waistband.

14   "Hold steady," he said. "I'll have to swing you out over the cliff."

15   With a powerful tug, he pulled Young out over the crevasse and held him dangling in midair. Then Muir swung Young toward him. As he did so he caught the collar of Young's shirt in his teeth.

16   "I've got to let go of you," Muir told Young through clenched teeth. "I need both hands now. Climb upward with your feet."

17   With that, Muir began pulling himself back up the steep slope.

ponder
think about

18   "How he did it, I know not," Young later declared. "The miracle grows as I **ponder** it. The wall was almost perpendicular and smooth. My weight on his jaws dragged him outwards. And yet, holding me by his teeth as a panther her cub and clinging like a squirrel to a tree, he climbed with me straight up 10 or 12 feet, with only the help of my iron-shod feet scrambling on the rock."

19   When they got to the top of the slope, Muir set Young down on the ground. Young was wincing with pain from his dislocated shoulders, but he was grateful to be alive.

20   Muir managed to shove Young's right shoulder back into place. The left shoulder could not be moved, however, so Muir used a handkerchief to make a sling for Young's left arm. Then the two men began the long climb back down the mountain.

21   First, they had to get down the wall of rock that Young had barely been able to climb up. In the darkness Muir took Young on his back and carried him much of the way. Three times Young's right shoulder popped out of place again. Each time Muir yanked it back into position.

22   Around midnight they reached the bottom of the wall. They still had 10 miles to go to reach the base of the mountain. Hour after hour Muir pushed, pulled, and carried Young along. Young later said that Muir did "the work of three men, helping me along the slopes, easing me down the rocks, pulling me up cliffs, dashing water on me when I grew faint with the pain."

23   At last, at 7:30 the next morning, the two men reached the bottom. Wrote Young, "The shoulder was in a bad condition—swollen, bruised, very painful." It took five men four hours of pulling before they were able to wrench it back into place. Even during that painful procedure, Young knew he was a lucky man. He had come within a few inches of death, but he had lived to tell about it.

If you have been timed while reading this article, enter your reading time below. Then turn to the Words-per-Minute table on page 121 and look up your reading speed (words per minute). Enter your reading speed on the graph on page 122.

Timed Reading

Reading Time: Lesson 3.4

_____ : _____

Minutes   Seconds

COMPREHENSION & CRITICAL THINKING SKILLS

A Recognize and Recall Details

Put an X in the box next to the answer that correctly completes each statement about the article.

1. John Muir wanted to climb the mountain quickly because he
   - ☐ a. wanted to prove he was a good climber.
   - ☐ b. wanted to reach the top by sunset.
   - ☐ c. wanted to challenge Young.

2. Young slid down the 12-foot slope because
   - ☐ a. his shoulders were weak.
   - ☐ b. he stepped too close to the edge and a rock slipped.
   - ☐ c. he could not jump far enough.

3. In order to reach Young, Muir had to
   - ☐ a. circle around the mountain.
   - ☐ b. jump back across the gap.
   - ☐ c. hang onto the wall with his chin.

4. As Muir and Young made their way down the mountain,
   - ☐ a. Young fainted from the pain of his dislocated shoulders.
   - ☐ b. Muir shoved Young's left knee back into place.
   - ☐ c. Muir pushed, pulled, and carried Young along.

B Find the Main Idea

One of the statements below expresses the main idea of the article. One statement is too broad. The other statement is too narrow—it explains only part of the article. Label the statements using the following key:

M Main Idea	**B** Too Broad	**N** Too Narrow

_____ 1. When S. Hall Young slid down a steep slope and dislocated his shoulders while mountain climbing, his friend John Muir had to make a daring rescue and help Young down the rest of the mountain.

_____ 2. S. Hall Young slipped down a steep slope while mountain climbing and had to hold onto the wall with his chin.

_____ 3. S. Hall Young and John Muir climbed mountains in Alaska.

C Summarize and Paraphrase

1. Reread paragraph 8 in the article. Below, write a summary of the paragraph in no more than 25 words.

   _____
   _____
   _____
   _____

   Now rewrite your summary in 15 words or less.

   _____
   _____
   _____

2. Choose the best paraphrase for the following sentence: "He was now hanging so far over the crevasse that any movement could send him to his death."

   ☐ **a.** He was leaning so far over the crevasse that he was afraid he would slip and fall to his death.

   ☐ **b.** He was hanging so far over the edge of the crevasse that if he moved at all he could fall to his death.

   ☐ **c.** He was so close to the edge of the crevasse that any movement could cause him to slip.

D Make Inferences

When you combine your own experience with information from a text to draw a conclusion that is not directly stated in the text, you are making an inference. Below are statements that may or may not be inferences based on information in the article. Label the statements using the following key:

C Correct Inference	**F** Faulty Inference

_____ **1.** Young had not told Muir that his shoulders were weak.

_____ **2.** Muir had already climbed many mountains such as the one that he and Young climbed.

_____ **3.** Young did not know that he would have to climb walls of rock on the hike with Muir.

_____ **4.** Muir was easily frightened.

_____ **5.** There were several hospitals available near the mountain that Young and Muir climbed.

E Recognize Author's Effect and Intentions

Put an X in the box next to the answer.

1. The main purpose of the first paragraph is to
   - ☐ a. give background information for the story.
   - ☐ b. entertain the reader.
   - ☐ c. describe S. Hall Young's experience climbing with John Muir.

2. What does the author imply by saying, "He didn't have much experience, but how hard could it be?"
   - ☐ a. Young thought he would need a lot of experience to climb a mountain.
   - ☐ b. Young thought he wouldn't need a lot of experience to climb a mountain.
   - ☐ c. Young thought the climb would be hard for anyone.

3. The author tells this story mainly by
   - ☐ a. retelling Young's personal experiences.
   - ☐ b. telling the story from different points of view.
   - ☐ c. using imagination and creativity.

F Evaluate and Create

Put an X in the box next to the answer.

1. Which of the statements below is an opinion?
   - ☐ a. Although climbing mountains can be dangerous, it is worth the risk.
   - ☐ b. With a powerful tug, he pulled Young out over the crevasse and held him dangling in midair.
   - ☐ c. Carefully Muir lowered himself down the slope toward Young.

2. Choose the statement that correctly completes this sentence: On the positive side, Muir was able to save Young, but on the negative side, _____ .
   - ☐ a. Young had been severely injured
   - ☐ b. Muir was not very brave
   - ☐ c. Young decided never to climb a mountain again

3. Young couldn't grab onto the wall with his hands because
   - ☐ a. his feet hung out over the crevasse.
   - ☐ b. his shoulders had been dislocated.
   - ☐ c. his hands had been crushed.

Unit 3 · Lesson 3.5

Killer Bees

Swarms of killer bees are capable of killing human beings. These bees are much more aggressive than ordinary honeybees, and when they get angry, they attack in large numbers.

Before You Read
Make Connections

Connect things you have learned or experienced about ordinary bees with the idea of killer bees.

- How can bees kill people?
- Why would bees kill people?

Killer Bees

1   Christopher Graves didn't have time to run away. One moment he was starting up his lawn mower and the next moment he was completely covered with angry, stinging bees. The attack came on August 23, 1994. Graves was at his grandmother's home in Texas. He had planned to cut the grass for her. When the 20-year-old Graves started the mower, he upset a swarm of bees in the area.

2   Graves saw the first bee come at him. He felt its sting.

3   "In the next blink of my eye," he said, "I was just covered."

4   Indeed, about 4,000 bees had appeared out of nowhere. They buzzed furiously around Graves. They stung him more than 1,000 times. Each sting carried just a small amount of poison. All together, the stings threatened his life. By the time firefighters arrived and got him to the hospital, Graves was in serious condition.

5   This was not the first time bees had attacked a human, and it would not be the last. In fact, since 1957, more than 1,000 people have been killed in bee attacks. **Countless** more have fought off angry bees and survived.

6   One survivor was 51-year-old Leonard Salcido. On August 16, 1997, he was mowing his backyard in New Mexico. Salcido knew there was a beehive in the fence at the edge of the lawn, but he wasn't worried about it. It had been there for a long time. In the winter, he and his family gathered honey from it. The noise of the lawn mower never seemed to bother the bees at all.

7   However, on this day the bees went crazy.

countless
so many that the number cannot be easily counted

8   "It was like a horror movie," said Salcido's daughter. "My dad was mowing the yard when we looked out and saw him running toward the water hose. I ran out of the house and grabbed the hose and tried to spray him down with water. The bees came for me. They were everywhere. The water was not getting them off my dad." By the time Salcido got away from the bees, he had been stung over 100 times.

9   Stories like Graves's and Salcido's are becoming more and more common. That's because there is a new kind of bee in America. Scientists refer to it as the "Africanized bee." Most people just call it the killer bee.

10   Long ago there were no honeybees of any kind in North or South America. Then, in the 1600s, Europeans brought some over. These European bees quickly **adapted** to life in North America. They set up colonies. They built hives and produced honey. However, these bees did not do so well in Latin America. They didn't care for the hot, **humid** climate. As a result, little honey was produced in Latin America. If folks there wanted honey, they had to ship it in from the North.

adapted
became used to

humid
damp or muggy

11   In the 1950s, scientists hoped to change that situation. They wanted to breed honeybees that liked hot weather. They knew that African bees did well in hot climates. However, African bees were much more aggressive than the European variety. They were more easily disturbed. When they got angry, they attacked in large numbers.

12   However, scientists thought the African bees could be helpful. They brought some to a laboratory in Brazil. They never meant to release the bees into the open. Instead, they planned to keep them locked away in the lab. There they could crossbreed them with European bees. In time, they hoped to get a new and

improved bee. It would not only have the gentle personality of European bees but also the African bees' love of hot weather.

13   It sounded like a good plan. However, something went wrong. In 1957 a group of African bees escaped from the lab. They flew out into the wild. Soon they began to take over local hives. They bred with European queen bees. The new Africanized bees certainly liked hot weather, but their personalities were far from **mellow**.

mellow
easygoing

14   "All honeybees have bad days," the scientist explained. However, for the new Africanized bees, every day was a bad day. These bees are 10 times as aggressive as European bees. It takes European bees about 19 seconds to get irritated enough to sting. It takes Africanized bees just three seconds.

15   That's not all. European bees will chase a person for only about 400 meters. Africanized bees will follow their targets for a metric mile.

16   Africanized bees work in large groups. People are rarely stung by just one or two. If these bees feel threatened, huge numbers of them immediately rush out to attack.

17   Could the news get any worse? Yes. Consider this: it takes just one Africanized bee to drastically change a whole colony of European bees. Experts think that's what happened in Leonard Salcido's case. One killer bee might have found its way into his peaceful backyard hive. In just 45 days, that one bee could have transformed the colony. Instead of European bees, the hive would have been filled with Africanized bees.

18   Experts point out that killer bees attack only when they feel threatened. So the key is to stay far away from them. That advice would have helped

Chisha Chang. On August 3, 1998, the 88-year-old Chang found a beehive attached to his barbecue grill. He thought he could remove it himself. So he put a plastic bag over his head for protection. Then he reached down to pull out the hive.

19 Suddenly, dozens and dozens of bees flew out at Chang. They swarmed all over him. Many got up inside the plastic bag. They stung him all over his face and head.

20 Police and firefighters were called to the scene. Said one firefighter, "I would describe him as having a hive of bees on his face. You could not see his eyes or his nose. It was like a hive being taken out of a tree and placed on his head."

21 A rescue worker managed to pull the bag off Chang's face and move him to safety. Luckily, Chang survived the attack. Later a specially trained beekeeper removed the hive from the grill. He **estimated** that it contained 70,000 bees.

estimated
guessed

22 Today killer bees are a fact of life in Texas, New Mexico, Arizona, and California. However, the rest of the United States doesn't have much to worry about. Africanized bees still love hot weather. Whenever they stray to colder regions, they die. That's good news—at least in colder regions—for anyone who likes to mow the lawn in peace.

If you have been timed while reading this article, enter your reading time below. Then turn to the Words-per-Minute table on page 121 and look up your reading speed (words per minute). Enter your reading speed on the graph on page 122.

Timed Reading

Reading Time: Lesson 3.5 _____ : _____
                             Minutes   Seconds

COMPREHENSION & CRITICAL THINKING SKILLS

A Recognize and Recall Details

Put an **X** in the box next to the answer that correctly completes each statement about the article.

1. Scientists who brought the killer bees to America had hoped to create a new kind of bee that would
   - ☐ **a.** be more aggressive than the honeybee.
   - ☐ **b.** do well in hot climates.
   - ☐ **c.** be gentler than the honeybee.

2. Scientists sometimes call the killer bee the
   - ☐ **a.** Africanized bee.
   - ☐ **b.** honeybee.
   - ☐ **c.** European bee.

3. A group of killer bees escaped from scientific laboratories in
   - ☐ **a.** Florida.
   - ☐ **b.** Brazil.
   - ☐ **c.** Mexico.

4. One reason why killer bees are more dangerous than honeybees is
   - ☐ **a.** the amount of poison each bee holds.
   - ☐ **b.** their inability to live in cold climates.
   - ☐ **c.** their aggressive nature.

B Find the Main Idea

One of the statements below expresses the main idea of the article. One statement is too broad. The other statement is too narrow—it explains only part of the article. Label the statements using the following key:

| **M** Main Idea | **B** Too Broad | **N** Too Narrow |

____ 1. Killer bees have been a serious problem in the southern United States.

____ 2. Killer bees, a cross between African and European bees, can be found in the hotter areas of the United States. They attack in swarms and are capable of killing human beings.

____ 3. Killer bees may chase their victims for a metric mile (six-tenths of a mile).

C Summarize and Paraphrase

1. Reread paragraph 17 in the article. Below, write a summary of the paragraph in no more than 25 words.

   _____
   _____
   _____
   _____
   _____

   Now rewrite your summary in 15 words or less.

   _____
   _____
   _____

2. Choose the best one-sentence paraphrase for the following sentence from the article: "This was not the first time bees had attacked a human, and it would not be the last."
   - ☐ a. The first time bees attacked a person, the attack did not last.
   - ☐ b. The second time bees attacked a person would be the last.
   - ☐ c. Bees had attacked people before, and they would attack them again.

D Make Inferences

The following inferences about the article may or may not be correct. Label the statements using the following key:

C Correct Inference	F Faulty Inference

_____ 1. One sure way to save someone from killer bees is to spray the victim with water from a hose.

_____ 2. Most people can easily outrun a swarm of angry killer bees if they are frightened enough.

_____ 3. Killer bees communicate with one another.

_____ 4. People living in areas in which killer bees are found should always avoid disturbing beehives.

_____ 5. Scientists will never be able to make killer bees less aggressive, even if they do more studies.

E Recognize Author's Effect and Intentions

Put an **X** in the box next to the answer.

1. The author uses the first sentence of the article to
   - ☐ **a.** inform readers about the danger of killer bees.
   - ☐ **b.** describe the personality of Christopher Graves.
   - ☐ **c.** make readers wonder why Graves did not have time to run away.

2. What does the author mean by the statement "Indeed, about 4,000 bees had appeared out of nowhere"?
   - ☐ **a.** The bees had the power to appear and disappear at will.
   - ☐ **b.** The bees appeared suddenly and without warning.
   - ☐ **c.** The victim had been sleeping and hadn't noticed the bees.

3. You can conclude that the author wants the reader to think that
   - ☐ **a.** the scientists should not have allowed any killer bees to escape because they caused so many problems later.
   - ☐ **b.** killer bees will eventually be replaced by honeybees, so there is nothing to worry about.
   - ☐ **c.** people cannot fight killer bees with any success, so people in southern states should consider moving north.

F Evaluate and Create

Put an **X** in the box next to the answer.

1. Which statement below is a fact?
   - ☐ **a.** There is nothing more painful and frightening than to be stung by thousands of bees.
   - ☐ **b.** The scientists who let the killer bees escape from the laboratory should be ashamed of themselves.
   - ☐ **c.** When killer bees get angry, swarms of them attack.

2. From the information in paragraph 22, you can predict that
   - ☐ **a.** killer bees will become a problem in the northern states.
   - ☐ **b.** killer bees will die out in the southern states.
   - ☐ **c.** killer bees will never be a problem in northern states.

WORDS-PER-MINUTE TABLE

Directions If you were timed while reading an article, refer to the reading time you recorded at the end of the article. Use this Words-per-Minute table to determine your reading speed for that article. Then plot your reading speed on the graph on page 122.

Lesson	1.1	1.2	1.3	1.4	1.5	2.1	2.2	2.3	2.4	2.5	3.1	3.2	3.3	3.4	3.5	Seconds
No. of Words	1231	890	1099	1048	850	1024	1097	1080	1051	1185	1002	985	1000	1124	1071	
1:30	821	593	733	699	567	683	731	720	701	790	668	657	667	749	714	90
1:40	739	534	659	629	510	614	658	648	631	711	601	591	600	674	643	100
1:50	671	485	599	572	464	559	598	589	573	646	547	537	545	613	584	110
2:00	616	445	550	524	425	512	549	540	526	593	501	493	500	562	536	120
2:10	568	411	507	484	392	473	506	498	485	547	462	455	462	519	494	130
2:20	528	381	471	449	364	439	470	463	450	508	429	422	429	482	459	140
2:30	492	356	440	419	340	410	439	432	420	474	401	394	400	450	428	150
2:40	462	334	412	393	319	384	411	405	394	444	376	369	375	422	402	160
2:50	434	314	388	370	300	361	387	381	371	418	354	348	353	397	378	170
3:00	410	297	366	349	283	341	366	360	350	395	334	328	333	375	357	180
3:10	389	281	347	331	268	323	346	341	332	374	316	311	316	355	338	190
3:20	369	267	330	314	255	307	329	324	315	356	301	296	300	337	321	200
3:30	352	254	314	299	243	293	313	309	300	339	286	281	286	321	306	210
3:40	336	243	300	286	232	279	299	295	287	323	273	269	273	307	292	220
3:50	321	232	287	273	222	267	286	282	274	309	261	257	261	293	279	230
4:00	308	223	275	262	213	256	274	270	263	296	251	246	250	281	268	240
4:10	295	214	264	252	204	246	263	259	252	284	240	236	240	270	257	250
4:20	284	205	254	242	196	236	253	249	243	273	231	227	231	259	247	260
4:30	274	198	244	233	189	228	244	240	234	263	223	219	222	250	238	270
4:40	264	191	236	225	182	219	235	231	225	254	215	211	214	241	230	280
4:50	255	184	227	217	176	212	227	223	217	245	207	204	207	233	222	290
5:00	246	178	220	210	170	205	219	216	210	237	200	197	200	225	214	300
5:10	238	172	213	203	165	198	212	209	203	229	194	191	194	218	207	310
5:20	231	167	206	197	159	192	206	203	197	222	188	185	188	211	201	320
5:30	224	162	200	191	155	186	199	196	191	215	182	179	182	204	195	330
5:40	217	157	194	185	150	181	194	191	185	209	177	174	176	198	189	340
5:50	211	153	188	180	146	176	188	185	180	203	172	169	171	193	184	350
6:00	205	148	183	175	142	171	183	180	175	198	167	164	167	187	179	360
6:10	200	144	178	170	138	166	178	175	170	192	162	160	162	182	174	370
6:20	194	141	174	165	134	162	173	171	166	187	158	156	158	177	169	380
6:30	189	137	169	161	131	158	169	166	162	182	154	152	154	173	165	390
6:40	185	134	165	157	128	154	165	162	158	178	150	148	150	169	161	400
6:50	180	130	161	153	124	150	161	158	154	173	147	144	146	164	157	410
7:00	176	127	157	150	121	146	157	154	150	169	143	141	143	161	153	420
7:10	172	124	153	146	119	143	153	151	147	165	140	137	140	157	149	430
7:20	168	121	150	143	116	140	150	147	143	162	137	134	136	153	146	440
7:30	164	119	147	140	113	137	146	144	140	158	134	131	133	150	143	450
7:40	161	116	143	137	111	134	143	141	137	155	131	128	130	147	140	460
7:50	157	114	140	134	109	131	140	138	134	151	128	126	128	143	137	470
8:00	154	111	137	131	106	128	137	135	131	148	125	123	125	141	134	480

Minutes and Seconds

PLOTTING YOUR PROGRESS GRAPH: READING SPEED

Directions If you were timed while reading an article, find your reading speed on the Words-per-Minute table. Then plot your reading speed on this graph by putting a small X on the line directly above the number of the lesson, across from the number of words per minute you read. As you mark your speed for each lesson, graph your progress by drawing a line to connect the Xs.

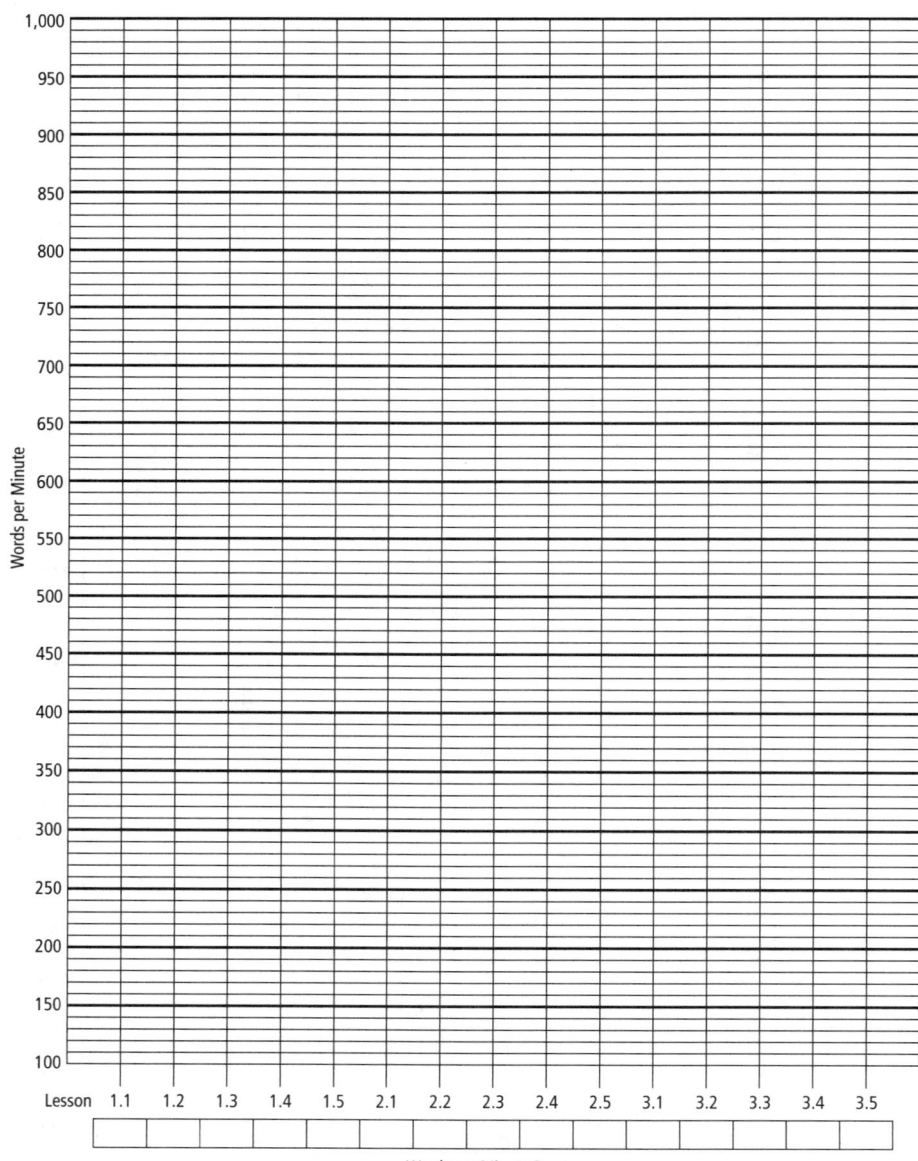